OTHER BOOKS by Julian Dutton

Keeping Quiet: Visual Comedy in the Age of Sound

'A custard pie in the face of those who say slapstick is dead, by the go-to writer of British visual comedy,' - Harry Hill.

Are We All Here? - a Journey through the world's most Curious Clubs.

'When the world seems to be doomed up pops Julian Dutton to assure you that all is not bad. Tears of joy are streaming down my face,' - Roy Gould, BBC.

Water Gypsies: a History of Life on Britain's Rivers & Canals

'A beautiful book. Julian Dutton grew up on the water, and he's the perfect guide to the life aquatic. There could be no better or more informative guide to a history of life aboard,' - Samuel West.

The Parade's Gone By: everyday life in Britain in the twentieth century.

'A history of Britain like you've never read before,' - History Now.

MY TOWN, MY RULES

The Diaries of Rowan Copernicus Battley
M.A., FSC,Qt., DoPe.

BRITAIN'S WIDEST COUNCILLOR
(Guinness Book of Records 2024)

Edited by Julian Dutton

First Edition published by Everyman Humour 2024.

British Library Cataloguing in Publication Data.
A catalogue record for this book is available from the British Library.

ISBN 978-1-3999-9161-2

Everyman Humour

CHADWELL TOWN (IDEALISED)

THE RIGHT HONOURABLE R. C. BATTLEY

(IDEALISED)

As I sit writing this in my garden office - a B&Q 12ft by 6ft Malvern Pavilion with pent-style roof and stylish glass-to-ground UPVC double-glazed windows, price £2,891.67 - I muse upon the magnitude of the achievement that lies in your hands.

Modesty forbids me from comparing these diaries with the august journals of Winston Churchill or Samuel Pepys. I shall leave that to others. The present volume is a 'warts and all' chronicle of the trials of civic leadership from 2019 to the present.

The question 'who am I?' can perhaps best be answered by asking 'who am I not?' I am not Fanny Craddock, the 1970s television chef. I am not many other people. I am Rowan Copernicus Battley, council leader of Chadwell, a small but thriving town in South Northamptonshire.

Four years ago I entered the modern age and launched myself on Twitter. No longer was I a remote figure to my beloved electors, but could inveigle myself into their homes and their brains twenty four hours a day, three hundred and sixty-five days of the year. This is something they wanted, and they have welcomed me into their hearts. The volume you hold in your hands is the harvest of these daily utterances - my triumphs, tragedies, laughter, despair, love, hate, wistfulness, ambition and eczema.

The public clamouring for the publication of my diaries has been relentless. At first I resisted the pleading - nay, the yearning - but from a spirit of selflessness, and the offer of a generous advance from a publisher, I finally yielded, and I offer them here to the nation on bended knee (I speak metaphorically - I haven't been able to kneel since Winsley Higgins attacked me during a particularly violent shove ha'penny match in 1978).

A word about myself. Councilling is in my bones. Apparently my first words were 'fiscal probity.' I have ~~ruled Chadwell~~ been elected council leader for thirty-five years, and have presided over my people with a velvet fist. My rise to power was perhaps inevitable, being part of the most notable dynasty of councillors in the South Northamptonshire region. My beloved parents, Dotty & Marmaduke, were councillors, as were their parents before them. In fact we can trace our family all the way back to Ethelred the Tediously Bureaucratic, Sheriff of Dunstable in 962ad and inventor of the first traffic cones, made from sheaves of wheat. It is not an exaggeration to say I live and breathe municipal administration. A permanent fixture on my bedside table is Mottram's *Local Governance,* written in 1932 but still the alpha and omega of councilling. I live with my wife Lola and my children Sally and Pericles in a modest 9-bedroomed house in the nice end of Chadwell. But I have never forgotten my humble roots - a modest 8-bedroomed house in the less salubrious part of town.

Which brings me to my beloved borough. The delightful little town of Chadwell nestles in the upper vale of South Northamptonshire as it abuts the sweeping chalk-hills of former Mercia. Vast Silurian gravel deposits laid down during the Jurassic era form the foundations of the earliest settlements, and it became a New Town in 1967. I realise I've left out a few things. Those seeking to learn more about our history are advised to consult *Market Chadwell - the first Billion Years,* by our Town Clerk Miles Cranford. Sadly Mr. Cranford only managed to complete volume 1, trailing off at 40 million BC. Driven insane by the magnitude of his task, he now resides in the Sunnylawns Care Home, dressed as a moth. He is forever in our thoughts.

The burden of power is weighty. Oft have I been crushed by the black dog of melancholy. It is one of the freedoms of the modern age that men are now permitted to speak openly about their feelings, and I can honestly say that there have been times when I've been really, really peeved. But I have soldiered on.

The aim of this little book is simple: to provide a record of the tumultuous times we have experienced during these last few years, but also to proffer a template, a guidebook – dare I say it a Bible – for all those seeking a life in municipal governance. Like Machiavelli's *The Prince*, it is a definitive handbook on How to Lead. These aren't my words. They are the words of Lulu, the Scottish popular singer behind such hits as *Boom Bang a Bang* and *Shout*. Lulu was briefly a resident of Chadwell in the early Seventies, and her support for me has never wavered. It is a source of great pride that she has furnished a delightful foreword to this humble volume.

FOREWORD

I lived briefly in Chadwell from 1971-1972 and Councillor Battley very kindly granted me planning permission for a loft.

Lulu

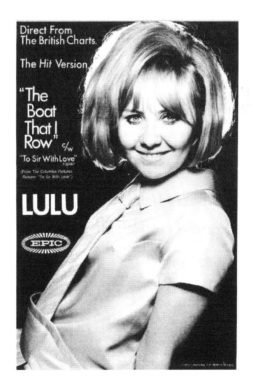

THE DIARIES

2019

August 1st
A bad beginning to the week. The council apologises profusely for shooting Ron Fossett today with a tranquilliser dart in the park, in the mistaken belief he was an escaped tiger. He was in fact doing a fun-run for Oxfam. This is particularly worrying as this is the second time he's been shot in 2 years.

August 3rd
Just returned from a splendid day judging the Women's Institute embroidery contest. A wonderful display of talent from local old folk! The day was sadly marred, however, by the winner, Edna Hulme, 89, testing positive for drugs. She was handcuffed, dragged off screaming, and her embroidery burned. Alarm bells should have rung when she produced this magic mushroom-fuelled monstrosity. There are bad apples in every walk of life I'm afraid, and the world of cross-stitching is no exception. The woman is a drug-crazed disgrace. I will let you

judge whether our diagnosis was just. This is just a sample of her textile work:

August 14th
The Council apologises unreservedly for the mural of General Pinochet unveiled today at Chadwell Infants School. It was of course meant to be Pinocchio. We've traced the culprit - it was Reg in the Dept. of Public Works. Handwriting atrocious. Make no bones about it, he's toast.

(The reader will note that these journals begin with apologies. I have no compunctions about this - it is the sign of a great leader

to take full responsibility for his ~~kingdom~~ borough. I learnt humility from Christ).

August 20th
Very successful manoeuvres today with the Chadwell Scout Troop! Pleased with our new Challenger 2 tanks. Of course the usual moaners from the Gazette were sniffing round asking 'why on earth does a scout troop own heavy artillery?' Well I have just one thing to say to that: jog on, numpties. When Kettering invades don't come crying to me.

August 23rd
Very pleased with the new council estate on Riverpark Drive. When I commissioned Transylvanian architects Dracula, Dracula & Winterbottom to design a 'fresh, innovative social housing development,' people scoffed. Scoff now, fu★kw★ts!

Sept. 3rd
It's come to my attention that the toad-crossing in Canal St. is being abused. Several frogs have been spotted using the facility. If you see a frog attempting to cross at this Junction tell them they have their own crossing 20 yards down the road. Otherwise it's f**king anarchy.

Sept. 13th
Ugly rumours are circulating of cheating at yesterday's Rotary Club Fete. I want it on the record that my wife Lola won the arm wrestling contest fair and square. She may look demure but make no mistake ten years of Zumba has given her the core strength of an orang utan.

Sept. 14th
Bulging inbox as per about my recent attempts to revive the High Street. I stand by my decision to grant licences to 14 brothels between the drop-in centre and the Harry Worth Memorial Hall

and anyone who challenges me will have to wrench my mayoral chain from my cold dead hands.

Sept. 15th

Yet more flak about the council's response to the recent floods. How many more times? – Nora in transport typed 'teabags' instead of 'sandbags' which is why four tons of PG Tips was delivered to the houses on Reservoir Drive. Move on, FFS.

Sept. 17th

The PC brigade triumphs again! It is with heavy heart that I have to announce that after 300 years Chadwell municipal gardens will no longer play host to the annual Thrashing of the Pensioner. Our beloved rack has been moved to the local museum. Dark times.

Sept. 18th

PARISH HALL NEWS: The Archbishop of Chadwell's lunchtime talk today in the memorial hall, 'How to Achieve the Perfect Orgasm,' is sold out.

Sept. 19th

Carnage at the Summer Fayre this afternoon. Placing the Bash-the-Rat stall right next to the display of pet rodents was an error ill-befitting the Fete Committee. Latest reports are 3 concussed hamsters, 2 gerbils in intensive care and a guinea pig with migraine. Heads will roll.

Sept. 20th
Seething. The council's been turned down for a lottery grant to develop the wasteland by the canal into a Slug Sanctuary. Apparently 'slugs aren't interesting.' Good mind to go to Lottery HQ and stuff 500 slugs through their letterbox, see if they find that 'interesting.' F★★kers.

Sept. 21st
Jjust returned from Chadwell Amateur Dramatic Society's opening night of Jurassic Park. Reverend Taylor was very convincing as a velociraptor, and Mrs. Portnoy took to the part of a Tyrannosaurus Rex with gusto. Hard to believe they're both in their 70's. Bravo to all!

Sept. 23rd
My wife Lola will be selling her crocheted dolls in the precinct this Saturday, all proceeds to the drop-in-centre. For God's sake buy one, she's made 200 of the bloody things. They're all over the house. Every time I open the airing cupboard it's like being attacked by Chucky.

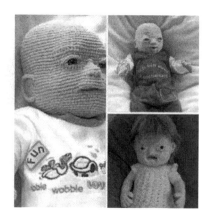

Sept. 23rd
FFS. Morning stroll in the Municipal Gardens with daughter Sally & son Pericles ruined by spotting a flowerbed spelling out 'Cllr Battley is a t**ser,' in geraniums. And all because I danced with the gardener's wife at the Welfare Club ten years ago. Let it go, Ambrose!

Sept. 19th
I hate you. Woken to a rammed inbox full of complaints about delays to the building of the ring-road.
Let me be clear.
Was the ring-road commissioned in 1972?
Yes.
How much of it has been built?
3ft-6 inches.
Why?
We forgot about it.
Now can we PLEASE just enjoy our evenings?

Sept. 25th
I swept to power on a zero-tolerance ticket. Today the Todd
Carty Playground witnessed this barbaric outrage of vandalism. I
at once mobilised all the resources at the council's disposal & after
a 10-hour manhunt the net closed on 3 yr-old Timothy Parker.
Make no mistake, Parker's going down.

Sept. 24th
Chuffed to bits that one of my Scouts, Tim Kip, was honoured
today for untying a pensioner in the Advanced Yoga class. 'I was
passing the village hall, heard the screams, and just put my
knotting skills in reverse,' quipped Tim, 15. One for the
Chadwell Bugle. Well done, Tim!

Sept. 17th
An update on Rev. Taylor who was arrested last night in a lay-by
outside Dixons in a compromising position in a Ford Fiesta with a
woman by the name of Busty Beryl. I have it on good authority
the Rev. was administering CPR to the said lady who suffers
from mild angina. End of.

Sept. 19th
Ugly rumours are circulating that the chute leading from my bedroom window to the adjacent open-air swimming pool is 'taking the p★★s.' As your leader I have to test every facility on a regular basis. I don't enjoy sliding gently into a warm pool every morning, but duty calls.

Sept. 26th
Woken as usual by tanks trundling past window - Chadwell WW2 re-enactment society starting early. Their aim - to re-enact the entire second world war from start to finish - beginning to grate on the town's nerves. Nearby streets strafed by Luftwaffe as I get milk in off doorstep.

Sept. 27th
To all those idiots who said Chadwell Sewage Farm could never become a successful theme park & weekend destination for thousands of tourists, eat humble pie, tw★ts. Rides, street-food, and all your favourite characters from the world of sewage dancing around in fabulous costumes. A triumph!
'The perfect day out,' - Princess Anne.
'I thought a sewage farm would not be good. I was wrong,' - Sting.

Sept. 28th
There are crazed rumours afoot that cannibalism is a solution to
climate change. Henry Fossett was strolling in the park when
someone tried to eat him. We're a new-town, not a dystopian
hell-hole from the Walking Dead! Let's build more cycle lanes,
not tuck in to our neighbours. Rant over.

Sept. 30th
I'm not in the councilling game for adulation, love, or fame.
Which is just as well as I'm currently having rocks thrown at my
Honda Civic as I drive through the Syd Little Estate. Any more of
this they'll be getting a visit from my good friends Mr. Water and
Mr. Cannon. T★★★ers.

Oct. 2nd
FFS. Much caterwauling & barracking in the chamber today
about my recent fact-finding mission to Saint Tropez. Is it my
fault the only fact I found was that it's a great place for a holiday?
They can jog on. They'll have to wrench my Kiss Me Quick hat
from my cold dead head.

Oct. 4th
Councillors have to make tough decisions. When the finance
department told me it was a choice between an oil painting of
myself, or free tea & coffee in the drop-in-centre for 20 years, I
wrestled inwardly for days. After much spiritual and moral agony,
I came to a conclusion. The portrait will be commissioned in a
few days.

Oct 6th
Disappointing turn-out for the Chadwell Scouts Sausage Supper
last night – just me, my Akela Mrs Riley and a chipolata under the
stars. Furious none of our cubs turned up. Discover this morning
it was 2-for-1 night at Laser-Quest. Well they can whistle for a
new flagpole. Bast★rds.

Oct 7th
VICTORY! To do our bit for the obesity crisis Chadwell Council's only granting planning permission for narrow houses, to encourage thin people into our borough. First development on sale this week. And please, no more letters to the Chadwell Argus denouncing me as a 'stupid fattist tw★t.'

Oct 8th
Neighbour Ralph Todd installs big new bird-bath in garden. To outdo him I fix a tiny towel-rail on mine, soap-dish, feather-conditioner, miniature sauna for stressed robins, &

power-shower. F★★★ing disaster. Turn shower on, eight wagtails blasted across garden. Slink indoors.

Oct 10th

WHOAH! Ok. I dislike traffic wardens as much as anyone, but sealing up Tony Smith in a Wicker Man is not the way to go. Thankfully he was rescued before it was lit, but he's visibly shaken & is recovering in the Vicarage with a large scotch. This the third time, and it ends now.

Oct 12th

Not impressed with this plan to tackle child obesity by banning eating on public transport. When my son Pericles ballooned to 40 stone we left him in the New Forest with a compass, a pac-a-mac & a capri-sun. He arrived home nine days later weighing 10 stone. Job done.

Nov 1st

Sunday stroll around the park ruined by caution from PC. Let me be clear. From the moment I took office I informed everyone I am a lifelong nudist. If a councillor can't strip naked and gambol round a municipal fountain then frankly I don't want to live in this country anymore.

Nov 3rd

FFS. I see my Wikpedia page has been vandalised again. Pathetic. Don't know why they do it - everyone knows I am the ★Rector★ of Chadwell University, not the 56'Rectum.' What even is a Rectum of a University?
Trouble sleeping now. Even my Horlicks is annoying me.

Nov. 4th

Today I took the difficult decision to dismiss Town Hall receptionist Helen Nuttall, on the grounds that she's a waxwork. I hold my hands up & admit I never noticed. I just thought she was very calm. Quite how she's managed to stay in her job for 15 years is, frankly, baffling.

Nov 5th
Seething. For the last time Enrico's Espresso bar in the High St. is a legitimate business and in no way connected to money-laundering. Sceptics question the £5m annual turnover. So we like espresso in Chadwell, deal with it! Enrico's a fine man, as are his 23 cousins from Palermo.

Nov 18th
Ok. The person who stole the ornamental cartwheel from outside the Fig & Trumpet last night and rolled it down Canal Street into the fountain - you're on CCTV, mate. We know who you are. So if you've sobered up, Reverend, just return it tonight and we'll say no more.

Nov 21st
Shocked to hear of the sudden death of Chadwell's most famous Australian explorer, Colonel Babberley-Swinnerton. He was attacked by kangaroos, head-butted by a duck-billed platypus then torn to shreds by a thousand koala bears. It's how he would have wanted to go. RIP.

Dec 6th
Once again the citizens of Chadwell salute the inhabitants of Pitcairn Island for sending us an annual Christmas tree in return for helping them in the War of Captain Jenkin's Ear, 1739.

Dec. 8th
Thanks to all who attended the turning on of the Xmas lights tonight, & a special thanks to Sandy Toksvig's half-sister for flicking the switch. And to those b★★st★ds moaning about the tree

– do one. You're lucky you didn't get a 40 watt bulb and a sprig of dead holly. F*** off.

Dec.9th

Devastated by the Russian sports ban. The council was really looking forward to welcoming Sergei Korsakov next Spring to our annual croquet tournament.

Dec 15th
Fantastic afternoon at Oddfellow's Hall for the Grand Christmas Sale of fetish wear. The gimp masks were flying off the trestle tables and I lost count of how many people walked out laden with whips, furry handcuffs & basques. All proceeds to the church roof restoration fund.

Dec 25th
Come one come all to Christmas Land, Chadwell High Street, behind Hobson's funeral parlour! Fun & games for all the family! And for those sceptics saying 'what about the rats?' - no charges were pressed and they've been declared rodent-free since November. See you there! MERRY CHRISTMAS!

2020

Jan. 1st.
Happy New Year! WE'RE HIRING! Have you got what it takes to be our new resident council ventriloquist? Mrs Bunt is retiring aged 101. To be honest we don't know quite why we have a council ventriloquist – I think it dates back to Mayor Harbottle, whose mental condition is a matter of record. For those interested, DM me.

Jan. 10th
Ignored in the Honours List once again. Charming. Were they not aware of my naked cycle ride to Kettering to raise awareness of vertigo? My sponsored hop around the park for Save the Haddock? The honours system is dead to me.
Jan. 14th

Chadwell police today seized drugs worth £14 million following a raid on Baxter's Cocaine Wholesalers Ltd., Rother St. The council always had its suspicions about Baxters (formerly Hard Drugs R Us). Now is not the time to ask who gave them planning permission. Let's just rejoice.

Jan. 11th
The council's thoughts and prayers are with Belinda Cook, who was knocked out today by a giant letter B that fell off the municipal library. Unfortunately as a result of being flattened she was unable to return her library book, so she will be fined. But get well soon, Belinda.

Jan. 19th
Carnage at a visit to Sunnylawns Care home. You lose *one* pet anaconda in a sheltered housing unit and all hell breaks loose. Usual pathetic cries of 'why did you bring a snake to a game of over-80's bingo?' Finally found Slinky under the bingo ball machine. Chill out, wrinklies! FFS.

Jan. 20th
Lunchtime stroll around the park ruined by caution from PC. Let me be clear. From the moment I took office I informed everyone

I am a lifelong nudist. If a councillor can't strip naked & gambol round a municipal fountain then frankly I don't want to live in this country any more.

Jan. 22nd
Sheesh. Apparently eyebrows have been raised about my betting council money on horses. Can I gently remind people it was I who in 2015 bet the entire annual budget on 'Flash Harry' in the 2.30 at Lingfield? How else do they think the drop-in centre got built?
And so to evensong.

Jan. 23rd
Just back from the vets. Poor Benjy a little overweight. Apparently pie, chips and mushy peas is 'no meal for an Iberian ribbed newt.' Pardon me for living.

Jan. 24th
I've recently taken up colouring and can confidently recommend it as an effective antidote to stress and a soothing balm to a troubled soul.

Jan. 25th
As part of my life-long commitment to re-wilding Chadwell, a wolf will be released into the shopping centre tomorrow between 1pm & 3pm.

Feb 10th
Chaotic scenes last night at the village hall. The monthly Cage-fighting contest was double-booked with Chadwell Budgerigar Society. The sight of Bruce 'The Maniac' Cortez tearing a birdcage apart and giving a half-nelson to a parakeet will haunt my dreams until the day I die.

Feb 23rd
I've written to the Prime Minister urging him to reject China's bid to build HS2 in 5 years and instead hire Rod Flock & Sons, Chadwell, who pledge to complete it in 12 months. And please don't judge them on this house - Rod was going through a messy divorce and he'd hit the sauce.

Feb 24th
Ugly rumours circulating of Russian interference in our Parish council elections. You disgust me. The day Putin sticks his nose in Chadwell's affairs is the day I toss my mayoral chain into a skip.

There is absolutely NO evidence - and I urge you to throw your full support behind our new Town Clerk, Cecil Winthrop.

March 13th
Very depressed. Receive curt reply to my letter to Downing Street proposing that the Govt. establish a Local Councillor Hall of Fame. 'Dear Mr. Battley, this is your 15th time of asking, and once again the answer is no.' Drowning my sorrows in the snug bar of the Happy Sausage.

March 14th
Big day tomorrow - NASA will be blasting Councillor Harbottle into orbit. Total cost of trip, £20 million. Usual grumblings of 'why are we doing this?' and 'why the hell is Chadwell New

Town twinned with the International Space Station?' FFS, move on. God speed, Councillor.

March 15th
Emotional afternoon. The council have agreed to my proposal to rename the alley between Hope Street & Shoe Zone, Battley Way. This means no fewer than 26 streets in Chadwell now bear my name, from Battley Crescent near the canal to Rue de la Battley in the Cafe Quarter. Humbled.

March 16th
PANDEMIC PANIC BUYING!! Right - any more of this and I'm declaring martial law. I've done it before and I'll do it again. Anyone spotted in the precinct carrying more than two family-packs of Andrex Classic White toilet roll will be mown down with a Gatling gun. Message over.

March 17th
Chadwell's annual folk-ceremony where we build a mountain of 100 tons of toilet paper in the park, set it on fire and dance, laughing, among the flames, will not take place this year for obvious reasons.

March 21st
URGENT: #PANDEMIC
At 12 noon the containment phase will end & become the delay phase. Between 12 noon & 1pm we will enter a state of contained delay and between 1pm & 2pm delayed containment. Those who have not contained their delay will - oh, just wash your f*****g hands.

March 22nd
#PANDEMIC Taking every precaution in the Battley household. Just walked into the living-room and found Mrs. Battley reading a history of China, so I've had her deep-cleaned.

March 25th
#PANDEMIC Mrs. Battley enters sixth day of self-isolation. Very proud of her. Anyone who can spend 144 hours locked in a garden shed with nothing but a jigsaw puzzle is a credit to us all. On my knees sliding a halibut under the door. Sounds of nibbling. Hope to God she hasn't gone feral.

March 28th
Following Italy's heartening practice of singing from balconies to keep spirits up, once again Mrs. Battley will be performing Wagner's Ride of the Valkyries from our bedroom window at 7pm. And neighbours - please don't throw cabbages at her like last night.

March 29th
Ugly scenes in the precinct today with people panic-buying shoe-repairs. One man re-soled his hush-puppies fourteen times. Giuseppe's run out of heels and you can't find laces in Chadwell for love nor money. This footwear madness must stop!

Mar 30th
Oh dear. Mrs. Battley's self-isolation enters a critical phase. Unlocked her room to find this. She'd escaped through the air-con unit. Managed to shoot her with a tranquiliser dart as she leapt the privet hedge, now soothing her to sleep with Mantovani. God help us all.

April 2nd

In line with government advice I've built a Meccano robot of myself. 'Battley 2' will be sworn-in at the Town Hall tomorrow and undertake all council duties in my place during my period of self-isolation. NB. Please don't just push him over.

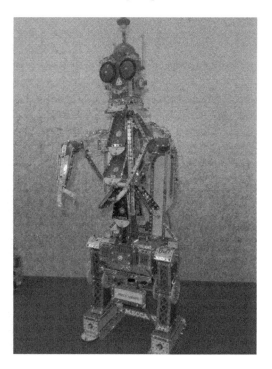

April 4th

Even during a pandemic life goes on, & I was thrilled to unveil this statue of myself outside town hall this morning. This will be 'placeholder' monument until the funds for a bigger one are approved. Naturally it was greeted with cat-calls of 'looks nothing like you!' etc. I sometimes wonder why I devote my life to serving such vile, worthless savages. Consoling myself in the Happy Fig.

April 5th

Ok, enough's enough. Not only were the shelves of Chadwell Superstore emptied today but the manager was stripped and someone ate his wig. And here's the Municipal Gardens this lunchtime. Does this scream 'social distancing' to you? Any more of this and you'll all be shot.

April 10th
Rigid with anger. Thought I'd do my bit for the current crisis &
spent all night in the garage making a ventilator. Govt. official
takes one look at it and denounces it as 'a pile of 'cr*p.' I'm the
first to confess I'm no medical engineer but a 'thank you' would
have been nice.

April 22nd
#LOCKDOWN Heartening to see Chadwell town centre totally
empty today. Well done everyone! Very proud of you.
Ah. Mrs. Battley's just told me the shopping centre's always like
that.
Still. Good.
Carry on.

April 23rd

Rumours afoot that a #ClapForBattley tribute is being arranged for tonight at 8pm, with everyone in Chadwell preparing to applaud my service to the town during this crisis. I really must protest – this shouldn't happen. It should be at 7pm, so Mrs. Battley and I can watch Question of Sport first.

April 26th

#LOCKDOWN To residents complaining that I ordered armed police to disperse a gathering of two hundred ants in Chadwell Municipal Gardens, pipe down and back off. How was I to know arthropods aren't included in the emergency measures? We need one thing from Government, and that's CLARITY!!!

April 27th

First day of home-schooling my beloved children Sally & Pericles. Somewhat aghast at my son's poor knowledge of maths. If he hasn't mastered Fermat's Theorem by the end of the day he can whistle for that rocking horse he wanted for his 4th birthday.

April 28th

Government ruling that only essential shops are allowed to remain open. Much controversy over my inclusion of Ron Bunt's Wigs for Pets Ltd. in Chadwell's list of vital retailers. Let me be crystal clear. The day I stop seeing a chihuahua trotting out of his emporium wearing a beehive hairpiece is the day I die.

April 29th

Yesterday, Chadwell's Chief Medical Officer Cinderella Dagenham stated that the coronavirus could be cured by a mixture of candyfloss & butterfly urine. After extensive tests in our laboratory we have found that sadly this is not the case. Miss Dagenham has since been sectioned.

May 2nd
Ok. I'm all in favour of home entertainment in these troubling times, but Bobby the Fire-Eater live-streamed his show from his living-room last night & took out half of Waterloo Crescent. My thanks go to the fire-service and to all those who had to evacuate. FFS stick to singing.

May 3rd
Do come along at 10pm to the Scout Hut in Polystyrene Lane where the Rev Bob Musgrove will be giving a 3-hour talk on his recent holiday to Swindon. Unfortunately the scout hut is being repaired so the talk will take place in the car-park. 2 metres apart, no refreshments. See you there.

May 6th
Ran out of cash last night so broke it to my three year old, Brenda, that the tooth fairy had been furloughed. Tough gig but every little helps.

May 7th
LOCAL ELECTIONS. When I first stood as councillor I asked the people of Chadwell to place their trust in me. They didn't. Why? I was only 6 years old. Many years later I stood again. They

handed me the crown. Today, they have done so again. I am weeping fitfully.

The work starts now. I'd like to thank my team & my beloved voters. As you know, Chadwell is twinned with Mustique. Tonight I fly out to my villa on Hummingbird Bay to work tirelessly, TIRELESSLY, on forging trade links with this great island. I'll see you in 2 weeks. I love you.

May 9th
Catatonic with fury. Found this tin of custard powder at the back of the cupboard and to my unfettered rage the contents have gone off! Dainty Maid Ltd. are refusing to reply to my emails. Admittedly mother bought it in 1936 but if I don't get a refund I'm switching to Birds.

May 11th
SOCIAL DISTANCING! WTAF? On my hour's exercise today, a jogger ran straight at me. I did what any sane person would do - I tripped him up, thrashed him with my walking-stick and rolled him into the municipal pond. And who gets told off by a passing constable? Muggins here! FFS

May 15th
I was determined to learn a new skill during lock-down so have added carpentry to my long list of accomplishments. Very pleased with this guillotine. It will only be used if martial law is declared, of course - but make no mistake, I will not hesitate to use it, and use it often.

May 16th
During the lock-down I thought I'd reconnect with Origami. Fond memories as a youth of making folded animals for Nanny. Wish I'd never bothered. Two hours later - 23 abandoned swans and a shredded flamingo. Crap.

May 17th
Disgusted. My neighbour's garden gnomes had a wedding this afternoon, flouting every social distancing rule under the sun. I'm very pleased to say the police have just rounded up the ceramic bastards. Hope they're all smashed to bits.
IF YOU'RE A GNOME - STAY AT HOME!

May 18th
Bombarded with emails from people who think if the economy shrinks by 14% then they too will shrink. My top advisers assure me that you probably won't, but to allay fears the council's set up a helpline: if you think you're shrinking, text HELPIMSHRINKING to 08002615348.

May 19th
Magnificent. Chadwell Council purchased 1000 of these robot dogs. Today they will roam the Municipal Gardens, the High

Street and the shopping precinct, and their laser-beams will kill anyone who isn't 2 metres apart. Have a lovely weekend everyone.

May 20th
Many queries about what's happened to the animals from Chadwell Zoo during the lockdown. Be assured they're all in good foster homes. Myself & Mrs Battley are putting up a couple of otters and Leslie from Trading Standards has an elk in her Granny flat. All is well.

May 22nd
Time to hold my hands up & admit the council's idea of giving Therapy Rats to Chadwell's old folk has simply not worked. To be blunt, it frightened the f***ing daylights out of them. I got the idea from therapy dogs and - well, now's not the time to play the blame game. Now is the time to treat the injured, and move on.

May 23rd
Mrs. Battley dozed off on a park bench during a break in our walk today. If that's 'Staying Alert' I'm a Dutchman. It was a tough call but I did what any fair-minded person in authority would have done. I summoned a constable and she was fined on the spot.

May 24th
IMPORTANT: The duck lockdown will not be eased until June 1st. How many more times? Anyone allowing their mallards out before that date will be shot. You think it's easy? You think I enjoy queuing outside my bathroom every morning behind six coots and a flamingo? Rant over.

May 25th
Council meeting on Zoom this evening. Catastrophe. Mrs. Battley walked in naked and proceeded to comb the bookcase behind me for a Catherine Cookson. Wolf whistles galore from Frank in Finance. Not a fitting end to a debate on pot-holes.

May 26th
My measures to ease the lock-down greeted by a typical volcanic sh*t-fest. Apparently letting lollipop ladies return to work before the schools re-open is, and I quote, 'stupid.' Oh really? Was it stupidity that swept me to power in a landslide in 1997? Jog on, morons.

May 27th
FFS. I see my Wikipedia page has been vandalised again. Pathetic. Don't know why they do it - everyone knows I am the *Rector* of Chadwell University, not the 'Rectum.' What even is a Rectum of a University? Ruined my day. Even my Crunchy Nut Cornflakes are annoying me.

May 28th
Things not going too well in the Battley household. Mrs. Battley & I not speaking. So many post-it notes festooning the kitchen it's like that bloody film Memento.

May 29th
Raging. The so-called 'artist' Franz Sieborg, from whom I commissioned a (second) statue of myself, has revealed his efforts.

Is this a joke? He says it's 'how he sees me.' Well all I can say is pay a visit to Specsavers, you beatnik c★★t.

May 30th

£"$£^^$%$%^$^?!!!!! WTAF? Six weeks of lock-down and this is what the Cilla Black Industrial Estate looks like. Chadwell is the Velcro capital of Europe, now look at us. Two words: Ron Pobble, Head of Maintenance. The man's toast.

June 1st
Disaster. My policy of issuing every resident a 2-metre long dachshund to ensure social-distancing backfires. Apparently there was carnage in the precinct as 500 sausage dogs ran amok. Two pensioners pulled along the ground like the bait in some ghastly drag-hunt. And so to bed.

June 3rd
Mrs. Battley and I planning a little holiday after all this has blown over. I suggested glamping in Glossop. She replied 'or caravanning in Canvey!' We both laughed.

June 4th
I'm very disappointed in you. Mrs. Roxburgh's wall was stolen this morning and she wants it back. Two men were seen scurrying down Chapel Lane lugging heavy bags. If you know the whereabouts of Mrs. Roxburgh's wall, text #IKNOWWHERETHEWALLIS to 0800783624.

June 5th
Catastrophe. At 2pm today the Assistant Mayor was spotted on the roof of the town hall screeching, jumping about & throwing things at passers-by. Obviously he had to be shot with tranquilliser dart. I feel it's time to hold my hands up admit it was a mistake to appoint a gibbon to public office.

June 6th
What a night. I discover that my gardener, Lassiter, whom I furloughed in March, has been sneaking in at night to tend to the flowerbeds. Spotted from my window, he looked up at me with plaintive eyes: 'But master, the perennials must be trimmed!' Naturally I set the dogs on him.

June 7th
No. 5 in the Council's Health & Safety Advice initiative: How to Survive a Plunge Down a Waterfall. Tomorrow, How to Survive in Space when your Helmet's Fallen Off. Good morning.

June 8th
FFS! Inbox rammed with complaints that the first business to re-open in Chadwell will be the sex shop. Let me be clear. I didn't spend ten years helping this town become the erotic capital of South Northamptonshire to see that smashed. Mrs. Beazley's Cave of Delights re-opens in June, end of.

June 10th
On this day in 1994 a preserved body was discovered in Chadwell marshes. Our very own bog person! Thousands flocked to see this stunning example of Iron Age sacrifice. Chadwell Man! Shame it turned out to be a shop window dummy, but for one glorious week we were on the map. Happy days.

★

June 11th

God this is exhausting. I repeat - drive-through psychiatrists WILL be open from next Monday. If you haven't got a back garden you CAN meet someone in your window-box, if they're less than 2ft-6ins tall. And you CAN attend a nail-bar, so long as your nails are 2 metres long. FFS.

June 12th

Good news, bad news. Bad news, I couldn't get Paul McCartney to headline the 'Let's-Go-Loco-for-the-end-of-Lockdown!' Festival in Chadwell Park on June 30th. The good news is, saxophone legend Dunk 'The Clown' Bedworth says if his eczema clears up, he's happy to step in.

June 13th

Another rammed inbox. I'm not saying this again. In England, 6 people can meet in a garden 2 metres apart. In Scotland, it's 8. If you have a relative who's half-Scottish, you can meet them in an English garden but at 4 metres apart and they have to be wearing a kilt. Simples.

June 14th
Drama over everyone! The whale that was stranded earlier today in the High St. outside Kwiksave has been transported safely back to the coast. Experts have deduced that it got into difficulty on the A63 and was probably confused by the one-way system. Panic over.

June 17th
You disgust me. No fewer than 17 swimmers were spotted today in the River Chad flagrantly flouting the social distancing rules. This is me patrolling the riverbed. I happily tased three people and punctured one man's lilo. Tomorrow I'm taking a 20ft harpoon. Be afraid.

June 18th
Very sad to learn of the passing of Dame Vera Lynn. Fond memories of Lynny when she opened Chadwell Fete in 1998. Naturally she sang for us. Looking back, I regret grabbing her microphone and launching into an acapella version of Smells Like Teen Spirit, but she enjoyed it. At least I think she did, she left halfway through. God bless. RIP.

June 19th
Lockdown easing taking effect. My cousin Ken and his wife Donna drove over from Uttoxeter today for a socially-distanced visit. Haven't seen them for months. As it happens we hate them so we hid behind the sofa & pretended to be out. But it was nice they had the opportunity.

June 20th
Remember, the horse lock-down ended today, so if you've been looking after a racehorse for 10 weeks, it's back to the paddock. Mrs B. & myself quite tearful as we bid adieu to Caramel Comet.

The queue for the bathroom was a pain and he cheated at Scrabble, but we'll miss him.

July 2nd
Exhausted. Just back from a Wake at the Railway Hotel. We were honouring the memory of one of Chadwell's finest sons – Wilbur Turnbull, inventor of the shopping trolley. By way of tribute we carried his coffin in a zig-zag fashion through the town then threw it in the canal.

July 3rd
As the supreme leader of our beloved town, whenever I wrestle with mighty decisions of state I seek wisdom from past great leaders. Currently reading the life of the Emperor Charlemagne. Unfortunately he has little to say on the subject of traffic cones, but it's a rattling read.

July 4th
I announced yesterday that there had been 140,000 Covid tests in Chadwell. Given our town has a population of 20,000, that is of course impossible. It turns out that we actually tested the same person 140,000 times. We apologise profusely to Mr. Kevin

Brown of 48 Dewlap Crescent, who is recovering in the vicarage with a large scotch.

July 5th
Very moving morning hosting Zoom meeting of the Chadwell branch of the National Society for the Prevention of Cruelty to Vegetables. We released three sprouts into the wild and Lottie Cowdrey moved us to tears with readings from her volume of poetry 'Mashed Potato is Genocide.'

July 6th
Cock-a-hoop. Just received a message inside my head. My son Pericles has won his Cub Scout Telepathy Badge!

July 10th
Gnashing teeth with rage. Scathing piece in the Chadwell Clarion denouncing my administration as 'old-fashioned.' WTAF?! Who employed Chadwell's first non-binary rat-catcher? Who cut the ribbon on the unisex toilets in the Reg Varney Drop-in Centre? Who invented interfaith Bingo?! FFS.

July 13th

FFS. Inbox jammed with flak from penny-pinchers after I unveil Chadwell's new public toilets. Yes, I modelled it on the Palazzo Monteverdi. Yes, it's lined with Tuscan marble. And no, it is *not* a 'monstrous waste of public funds.' Any other questions? Good because I'm a busy man.

July 18th
Praise God dentists are re-opening! Mrs Battley's bicuspids have become the stuff of nightmares. She's not talking to me atm, not because we've fallen out but because I took her teeth out last week. Don't blame me - blame 'Home Extraction Made Simple' by Don Fox. Not a good book.

July 19th
Seething. Mrs Battley & I attended a 70's-themed Zoom Party. Utter catastrophe. There we were, sitting in our hippy wigs and kaftans, only to discover it was meant to be the 1570's. Every other b★★★ard wearing a ruff. Left party early, now watching Flog It.

July 24th
Major announcement! With zoos re-opening but schools staying closed, from July 1st all children will be taught in zoos. Chadwell Zoo has a very clever gibbon who'll teach history, & an ex-circus pony brilliant at maths. And any moaners who say 'this is insane,' I'll hate you.

July 25th
I am not ashamed to confess that I am experiencing the first pangs of lockdown fever. But last night on an impulse I stepped naked into my front garden & launched into an interpretive dance. My soul broke open! Unfortunately my head broke open too after my neighbour threw a vase at me. But for a brief spell I dwelt with the angels.

July 26th
FFS. Wake to yet another rammed inbox. Chaos in village hall night as the Knitting Club was double booked with the Thai Cuisine Society - Mrs. Simms knitted a scarf out of egg noodles and Mr. Enstridge was rushed to hospital after choking on a sweet and sour cardigan. And so to whist.

July 27th
Storms wreak havoc on Chadwell! Just been told 15-year's worth
of rain fell in one second on the head of Keith Bunt, out walking
his dog. According to witnesses he was 'driven into the ground
like a tent-peg.' A crane is hoisting him to safety. Stay safe,
Chadwellians!

July 28th
I've been advised by my social media team that I'm swearing too
much on my twitter-feed. I've been reminded that I am 'the
public face of Chadwell New Town,' and as such should show
decorum, politeness, and positivity. What a load of old
f&★£$%^&★ing&^%ite^%$"£$R^ollocks.

August 1st
The council apologises for today's 19-mile tailback on the
Porlock Road. This was caused by the new tortoise-crossing at

Fossett Wood. Apparently a snail was using it, in flagrant contravention of the rules. The mollusc has since been arrested, and the road is now clear. Enjoy.

August 2nd
Here we go again. It's good old 'rake up the past' time. READ MY LIPS! When I invited Kim Jong-Un to open the extension to the cottage hospital, I DIDN'T KNOW WHO HE WAS!! Of course I was shocked when I found out. Not half as shocked as I was when the bloody fool turned up.

August 4th
Inspired by China & Hong Kong's 'one country, 2 systems' policy, as of today Chadwell will be 'one town, 19 systems.' The High Street will be communist, the shopping precinct neo-liberal, Depot Street to Oildrum Lane will be fascist, and the Municipal Gardens anarcho-syndicalist. Enjoy.

August 5th
PANDEMIC TRAVEL RESTRICTIONS.
Spot of confusion over where and where you can't travel. Let me be clear. You *can* go to San Marino but you can't come back, Latvia ditto. Peru, Lesotho, & Kuala Lumpur – you can fly over them but can't look at them, and if you go to Chad you'll be executed. Thank you.

August 7th
FFS. Just had BBC Panorama on the 'phone. They're planning to expose 'archaic practices' at Chadwell Hospital! Let them, that's what I say! I'm proud of our public gallery in the operating theatre – spectators have been witnessing operations since 1823. I personally had my gallstones removed last year in front of a packed house. I have fond memories of staggering to my feet in my hospital robes and taking three curtain calls. Long may it continue.

August 6th
Well someone's enjoying the end of lockdown. Go to feed cat this morning – nowhere to be seen. Search neighbourhood – find him off his head in the snug bar of the Ram & Fig. Carrying him back home now as he sings bawdy songs.

July 6th

Tragic news. Chadwell's biggest superstore, World of Thimbles, is to close. CEO Todd Bunter said it's nothing to do with the pandemic: 'Quite simply, people hate thimbles. Since opening 50 years ago we've sold a total of 23. I've wasted my life,' added the inconsolable magnate.

July 7th

Humbled! The Council's Resident Poet, Melissa Swan, has written a beautiful Ode chronicling my achievements. Entitled 'Is This Man a God in Councillor Form?' will be read at the Town Hall & streamed live. Such a surprise! Well not completely, as I commissioned it, but – great.

July 8th

Ecstatic! As Chairman of Chadwell's world-famous Biscuit Museum I'm thrilled to announce that we've acquired a ship's biscuit from 1784! Come & see our collection! We now have an Anglo-Saxon Hobnob, a custard cream signed by Hitler, Clint Eastwood's Minty Viscount, and many more!

July 10th

A splendid day in the history of our town! As you know Chadwell is twinned with Las Vegas, and today the Mayor Giancarlo Bruto and his lawyer Luigi surprised us all with a cultural exchange visit. He asked to see our casino so I showed him the fruit-machine in the Grouse & Goose.

He seems to love Chadwell, though he advised us to turn the drop-in centre into a Golden Nugget Blackjack Palace. As a parting gift he gave me a Kaloshnikov 22 automatic assault rifle, a snub-nosed Smith & Wesson, and some crack. I gave him a jar of Mrs. Battley's mango chutney. A very happy day. Here he is enjoying a tour of the OAP's Knitting Club in Thimble Lane –

July 11th
WTAF? Torrent of complaints about this month's itemised council tax bills: Police, Education, Recycling, & Cllr Battley's hand-woven ermine robes & jewellery. Problem? What do you expect me to wear for the grand re-opening of the cottage hospital, my f★★★ing underpants? JOG ON, CRETINS!

Juy 12th
Big night tonight! I'm the guest of honour at the Chadwell Beekeeper's Annual Dinner-Dance. As ever the location is kept

secret - at 7pm the President directs us to the venue by performing a ritual dance in the middle of the High Street.

July 13th
Very important in these uncertain times to support local restaurants. I've been doing my bit by having four of these a day at Fat Bob's Guzzle Shack. I'm now 18 stone and I was brought home yesterday in a wheelbarrow, but by God I'm determined to re-inflate the local economy.

July 14th
Well it was Carpet Madness down at Chadwell Floor Coverings Sale today! No, seriously, the manager Ron Ludlow had a mental breakdown and ran amok with an axe. Our thoughts are with his staff, all of whom thankfully escaped.

July 15th
FFS. Read my lips! Our allotments are there as a haven of peace & tranquillity for the citizens of Chadwell. But a few bad apples HAVE to spoil it for the rest of us by growing man-eating plants. Now I swept to power on a libertarian ticket, but six deaths a month? Unacceptable!

July 16th
It's with heavy heart that I have to announce the council will be implementing staff cutbacks. We will of course be focusing only on jobs that have become outmoded. I can't reveal anything more at present, apart from to say there's a question-mark hovering over the Witchfinder General.

July 20th
Wonderful birthday party today at Sunnylawns Care Home for Chadwell's oldest resident, Edna Pilbury, 112. What a plucky woman! We even gave her the bumps.

July 20th
RIP Edna Pilbury. Her last words – 'For God's sake stop giving me the bumps you f★★★ing idiots!' will be forever engraved on our hearts.

July 21st
ON THIS DAY IN 1848 local man Frank Flump accidentally poured sugar & starch into a vat of fusilli. The result was

surprisingly delicious, and the Flump was born. Chadwell still produces 19 million Flumps a day, and we are rightly known as the Flump capital of South Northamptonshire.

July 22nd
A very sad day in the history of our town. We say farewell to one of Chadwell's most famous entertainers, Monica Bledlow – wife, mother, and magician's assistant to the Great Verdini.

July 23rd
Disaster last night at the Cirque de Chadwell, when a socially-distanced trapeze act went horribly wrong. 'At the last minute we realised we're not allowed to catch each other,' said one of the Flying Tortellinis. Luckily Sid Tortellini plunged 100ft into a safety net, but it was red faces all round.

July 24th
A momentous day in the history of Chadwell's sewage system! After 10 years, Chief Rat-catcher Bob Stokes – the Captain Ahab of rodent infestation – has cAugustht the legendary sabre-toothed rat of the north drains, the same rat that chewed his leg off a decade ago. God speed, Bob!

July 25th
Much speculation that the trend with the hashtag
#CllrBattleyShouldbeMayorforLife was started by me. *Sigh.*
Does it really matter who started it? Wasn't it Buddha who said
the Self is an illusion & we are all one? So, according to Buddha, I
didn't start it – we all did! End of.

July 26th
FFS. Deluge of complaints about my weekly stint at Chadwell
Hospital Radio. Apparently pumping 3 hours of industrial
death-metal into the convalescent ward is 'not conducive to
patient well-being.' My response? Swivel, f★★★wits! My show,
Friday Night is Thrash Night, continues.

July 27th
Ensconced in the Mayoral Box at Chadwell FC. I know the
aggregate scoring in this championship is a tad confusing, but just
remember, if Chadwell score just one goal against the Uttoxeter
Rockets & Pevensey Bay beat Ironbridge by 3-2 then Chadwell
win the Hellespont League! In algebraic terms, C+2(-48.3 x
Uttoxeter)=24L-60%(Ironbridge). Simples. Go Chadwell!

July 28th
Just back from the Pet Club AGM. What a cluster-f★★k. What moron decided to put a bowl of twiglets next to the open display of stick-insects?! I will never forget the owners' screams as pet after pet was munched in the belief it was a marmite-flavoured snack. May God be with you.

July 29th
Weeping with joy. After years of bitter conflict at Chadwell Allotments, a ray of light has appeared in the form of new chairman Gus Enstridge. Gus has just announced he supports both vegetables AND rose-growing, ending 10 years of violence in which hundreds have died. #Lovewillwin

August 1st
What a day. The world's press descend on Chadwell after a local man claims he sees the face of Jesus in a biscuit. Bloody thing turned out to be a jammy dodger. Bishop of Rome flew in, took one look at it, stormed out, cassock flapping. Talk about embarrassing. And so to golf.

August 2nd
Thrilled to unveil Chadwell's new Theme Park. The theme is
'existential despair.' The park will be open 9am-6pm Mon-Sat,
exc. Bank Holidays & religious festivals. Enjoy.

August 3rd
On this day in 1971, Chadwell Council took delivery of its first pocket calculator. Happy days.

August 4th
Fantastic night at the British Legion celebrating the 102nd birthday of one of Chadwell's finest sons, Mortimer Bucklea, who during the Blitz won the Luckiest Baker of the War Award.

August 5th
CORRECTION: In last week's Council Newsletter it was stated that Mrs. Green of 38 Bridle St. was 'the most despicable human being ever to walk the earth.' It should have read 'She is Chairwoman of the Chadwell Knitting Guild.' For this minor typographical error we express regret.

August 6th
Here at the Council we are following strict Government guidelines on the size of meetings, and operating stringent safety measures. This has led to me implementing the rule that official meetings should not exceed one person.
Today I had a meeting with myself about Belisha Beacons. At one point tempers became frayed and I threw myself out of the room. But common-sense prevailed, I listened to myself, and approved two new beacons. Job done.

August 7th
Laying out the buffet for the Church Fundraiser. Jesus H. Christ. I ordered cocktail sausages. What do I get? Pork rectums. Do they honestly think the Bishop of Worcester's going to wrap his gnashers round a pig's arse? I might as well dance around him singing 'I love Satan.' FFS.

August 8th

Council guidelines on official meetings now getting a tad tricky. As the maximum number at any meeting is now one, the quorum is half a person. As my legs were at the meeting we reached the quorum & the meeting took place. Yesterday the Treasurer left his arms at home so couldn't meet himself to approve the budget. Difficult times but the council will rise to the challenge.

August 9th

A sad day in the history of the Battley household. We were entertaining the Vicar for high tea when he asked if he could feed our tropical fish. Before I could scream 'Stop, they're piranha!' he was dragged in and stripped to the bone.
It's how he would have wanted to go.

August 10th

Enough's enough. Following the Bishop of Chadwell's arrest last night in a lay-by in the arms of 'Madam Fifi,' the council has fully accepted his explanation that he was holding a very small Tarts & Vicar's Party in his car to raise money for the drop-in centre.

Now back off. The man's got a withered arm. Have some respect.

August 11th

For a staycation that can't be beaten, choose Chadwell New Town this August! Visit our Satanic Temple, our Museum of Slippers, and our unspoilt bypass. Guided tours of the Tyre Depot & the Flump Factory. We cater for all pockets from Hotel Splendide to Old Ma Biggin's Flophouse. Come one, come all!

August 12th

In the first of an occasional series, Chadwell Then & Now, I present the shopping precinct in 3000bc & 2020. According to archaeologists the woman is sitting in the entrance to Betfred, the man is driving his sheep through Shoe Zone, & the hut in the distance is now Ann Summers.

August 13th

MAJOR ANNOUNCEMENT!!! Fat Bob's Guzzle Shack on the bypass will no longer be able to serve its complete Imperial Belly-Buster Breakfast owing to lorry-driver shortages. From tomorrow it will contain only 4 eggs, instead of the usual 24. Steady, Chadwell. We can get through this.

August 15th

Very chuffed. My initiative to make local senior citizens feel more useful in the community is proving a resounding success. I've got three 98-year olds currently resurfacing my driveway, and they're loving every minute. Exhausted, yes – but deep down I know they're happy.

August 16th
I've made no secret of my devotion to nudism. Yet my stroll round the park this evening was RUINED by a caution from a passing constable. If a councillor can't strip naked & dance round a municipal fountain in the moonlight, frankly I don't want to live in this country any more.

August 17th
Our neighbours Ichabod and Phyllis over for drinks. A happy afternoon leafing through family snapshots. Here's my grandmother Tabitha. At only 3ft 6 she was the smallest councillor in the South Midlands but by God she knew her bye-laws.

August 18th
URGENT: as the llama strike enters it's third week, from 6 o'clock tonight I shall be calling in the army to provide essential llama services. Make no mistake, these furry anarchists will be

broken. Remember who smashed the Sloth riots of 1998? Trust me.

August 19th
Just back from the opening night of Chadwell Pet Club's production of The Importance of Being Earnest. Mr. Enstridge's stick insect was an interesting Algernon but Fifi the chihuahua's Lady Bracknell stole the show! Mrs. B. & myself were giggling fit to burst. A happy evening.

August 20th

Thrilled to see my old mate Knuckles Winthrop released from prison today. And please, let's not rake over the past ('he's a crook, he stole £1m of public money & fled to Benfleet!' - yawn yawn). Let's all just move on and welcome him back with open arms as Chadwell's Deputy Director of Finance.

August 21st

URGENT WARNING TO CHADWELL RESIDENTS: This harmless-looking creature is not as it seems. It's actually notorious con-man Roger Carstairs. He's been going door-to-door disguised as a Quokka, preying on elderly householders and fleecing their bank accounts. DO NOT APPROACH.

August 22nd
I'm sorry to have to announce that the prehistoric art discovered in Chadwell Cave has been declared 'inauthentic.' A representative from the Natural History Museum examined it and - well, he swore at me and stormed off. Very picky, these officials - can't see any problem myself.

August 23rd
Sick to my stomach. Our neighbours the Cottrells asked us to water their indoor plants while they're on a sketching tour of the Mendips. What do I see on their wall? - a dartboard with my face on it & 'Battley is a wa*ker' in felt pen. WTAF? Sponge your own sodding aspidistra!!!!

August 25th
Disgusting scenes in the park today from the Chadwell Prehistorical Re-enactment Society. In a pitched battle between Neanderthals & hominids there were 23 injuries, culminating in the Vicar dressed as an Australopithecus being airlifted to Chadwell General. This weekly carnage ends now.

August 26th

Evening stroll through the park. How I love this town! I passed the Rowan Battley bandstand & the Battley Pavilion. As I ambled home I realised there are no less than 23 streets in Chadwell named after me! Felt so humbled that I sat on a bench outside the Battley Theatre & wept.

August 27th

Okay, just ca-alm down everyone. Breathe. God knows how it happened - the council planning dept. obviously took its eye off the ball - but rest assured the new cafe in the High Street -'Hitler's Tea Rooms,' - WILL have its name changed by tomorrow.

August 28th

Thrilling day! Led my scout-troop in a re-enactment of the storming of Mafeking. We used old Jim Todd's house as the enemy fortress, inflicting a brutal attack with bows & arrows & air-rifles. Only problem was no one had told him. He's under heavy sedation but thankfully stable.

August 29th

#TRAVELBAN To circumvent the current restrictions on foreign travel, for our holiday this year I've converted the spare bedroom into the Maldives. I used some bags of sand from B&Q and the trees were supplied by Chadwell Garden Centre. Bit of pond-water, cunningly placed mirrors, bish-bosh, job done. Hard to believe the room's only 8ft x 6.

Sept. 1st

EMERGENCY! Following the discovery that the entire High St. is made of asbestos, I have declared a state of emergency. The council has erected 1500 tents in the park for evacuees. I shall be monitoring events from the penthouse suite of the Four Seasons Hotel. Good luck everyone.

Sept. 2nd

FFS. Usual moaners asking why the council has just bought its own Lear Jet. Get with the programme, sheeple! I shall be working tirelessly to sell our beloved town across the globe. Which is why tomorrow I'll be flying off on a fact-finding mission to the Maldives. Just rejoice.

Sept. 3rd

As everyone knows a council is only as good as its fax machine. It distresses me beyond words to announce that our beloved 1972 Magi-Fax has spat out its last sheet. Goodbye, my darling. We had some good times. It will be buried tomorrow in the presence of the Bishop of Chadwell.

Sept. 4th

In light of current sensitivity surrounding public monuments, Chadwell Council has come to the conclusion that the giant statue of Satan in the shopping precinct should perhaps be removed. I think it dates back to Mayor Harbottle, to be honest, whose schizophrenia is well documented.

Sept. 5th

Jesus wept, not this again. For the last time Chadwell does NOT have an Area 51. The council has NOT been keeping an alien in a depot behind the gasworks for the last 20 years. And this is NOT an extra-terrestrial - it's Alan Musgrove , who went strange after his wife left him.

Sept 6th
As we know Chadwell is the sex capital of the West Fens. As part of Erotica Week, yesterday I dressed up as a phallus & walked through the shopping centre. I was set upon by a gang of boys & rolled down Church Lane. Read my lips: when I dress up as a phallus, I demand respect.

Sept. 7th
Once again I submit plans for my new town hall. 6 acres of offices, pool, gym, as befitting a leader of my calibre. Do you seriously expect me to run my empire from this breezeblock monstrosity? We're the only council in Britain with an outside toilet! Give me the money!!!!

Sept. 8th
I have deleted yesterday's tweet about my political opponent Ted Burlap. I would like to state that I do not want to 'throw him into

a threshing machine,' or 'baste him in honey, stake him out & let the ants get him.'

Tempers can get frayed in politics. Let's put this behind us.

Sept. 9th
Ok. Deep breaths.
Did the council demolish Mrs. Tina Bun's house today in the mistaken belief it was in the path of #HS2?
Yes.
Is Chadwell anywhere near the #HS2 route?
No.
Why did you demolish it?
We don't know.
Will she accept a £50 book token as compensation?
I hope so.

Sept. 13th
When I swept to power in 1995 I made no secret of my devotion to naked wrestling. An online video is circulating of me in 1989 going 3 rounds with Albert the Giant. Let me be clear. We all have hobbies. Some of us refurbish penny-farthings. I fight nude people. End of.

Sept. 14th
You s*ds. Deluged with complaints about my playlist for last
night's hospital radio show at Chadwell General. If I want to play
14 tracks from my wife's self-produced album of Tyrolean folks
songs I'll bloody well play them! Get your own show! Tonight
she'll be singing live for 4 hours - deal with it.

Sept. 15th
FFS! If I've told the Signage Dept. once not to hire Sid Woodall
& Sons I've told them a thousand times. All over the town - 'Give
Weigh,' 'No Entree,' 'Buss Top.' Bloody pi**heads! This town's a
laughing stock. I'll see you in court, Woodall!

Sept. 16th
Thrilled to present the awards tonight at Chadwell's Average Citizens of the Year. Winners were Ron Brown, whose new paper shop is not too bad, Sally Turner, whose front garden is dull but presentable, & lollipop lady Fran Wilkes, who sometimes forgets her lollipop but she's ok.

Sept. 17th
With trembling heart & untold happiness I announce the completion of our town's finest tourist attraction - the Great Pyramid of Chadwell. Straddling the western edge of the Municipal Gardens, when my soul departs to heaven I will be mummified & interred within its sacred space.

Sept. 18th
As your beloved leader I must echo the Prime Minister's words regarding the new Covid-19 safeguards just announced. So remember... #HandsFaceSpace. Or, for Chadwell's thriving & valued cockney community - Brighton Sands, Boat Race, Cannock Chase. Thank you.

Sept. 19th
URGENT: Reports are coming in of fake £1 million pound notes being passed in local shops. This morning a man bought a packet of fruit pastilles from Mrs. Barnshaw's sweetshop and she had to give him £999,999 change. 'I've been a f***ing idiot,' she said, 'I'm ruined.' BEWARE!

Sept. 20th
WTAF? When I allowed a TV crew into our home for 6 weeks I did NOT sanction it being spewed out on local cable channel ChadVision entitled 'Keeping Up with the Battleys!' Half an hour

of me asleep on the couch? Mrs. B. doing naked Zumba on the patio?! I'll see you f★★★ers in court!

Sept. 22nd
Thrilled to announce that in conjunction with #ExperienceUnlimited I'm offering a day out with me for £49.99! Vote with me in the chamber! Cut the ribbon at a shop opening! Join the Chadwell Naturists as we dance naked in the park! (not compulsory, but everything's on the table).

Sept. 23rd
FFS. I've been told by the Tourist Board to remove the above picture from our website as - shock horror - it's 'not Chadwell.' NO ONE SAID IT WAS, M'F★★★RS! The caption clearly reads 'Chadwell is a beautiful town - LIKE Amalfi.' Jesus.

THIS is Chadwell. Happy now?!

Sept. 24th
Jesus Mary Mother of God. When Mrs. Battley said she'd
embarked on a course of Primal Squeak Therapy, I took it in my
stride. Sounds coming from the bedroom like a nest of
horror-stricken ferrets. I'm off for a walk.

Sept. 25th
I'm sobbing as I write this. The South Pole has finally normalised
relations with Chadwell. Ever since 1997 when I declared
Antarctica was part of Northamptonshire, things have been a tad
strained. No longer. I reach out & grasp every flipper of our
beloved thriving King Penguin community.

Sept. 26th
You barbarians. That's the last time I do an 'Ask Battley' session
on Zoom tackling the major issues of the hour. What questions

do I get? 'Who's your favourite Wacky Races character?' 'Have you ever been to Swindon? 'Do you like toffee?' TIMEWASTING BAST★★★DS!
And so to cribbage.

Sept. 27th
Not again. Ron Ellis's wild boars have got out. They're heading down Bancroft Rd. to the precinct. One's cornered in BetFred and another's eaten a dress in Dorothy Perkins. EVERYBODY IN!

Sept. 28th
Thrilled with today's #JapanTradeDeal. As you know, Chadwell is the Flump capital of East Mercia. And by God, as sure as my middle name is Copernicus, if we all put our noses to the grindstone we'll have everyone in Tokyo gorging on Flumps before Christmas. Let's do this.

Sept. 29th
And so the recession strikes Chadwell. With heavy heart I announce the closure of Uncle Jim's Flea Circus. The fleas have

taken it very badly – drunken scenes in the town centre, beating up ants etc. But rest assured, each flea will be offered an apprenticeship. We'll beat this.

Sept. 30th
If one thing civic life has taught me, it's humility. Which is why I refused to put my name on our magnificent Chadwell leisure centre – containing the Battley Pool, the Battley Theatre & the Cafe de la Battley, and surrounded by flowerbeds of beautiful Rosa Potente Battleyatus.

★

Oct. 1st
The council apologises on behalf of Ted Padstow for firing at three Messerchmitts this morning as they flew over Chadwell piloted by members of the Vintage Aircraft Society. Ted claims he 'had a weird flashback to 1940,' – which is a trifle strange as he was born in 1963. Quite why he has a M270B1 anti-aircraft gun in his back garden is not known.

Oct. 2nd

Not strictly council business but Mrs. Battley says she'll be selling her knitted snails in the precinct tomorrow – all proceeds to Cure Vertigo Now. She's knitted 68,000 of these bloody things. For the love of God please buy one because quite honestly I fear for her sanity.

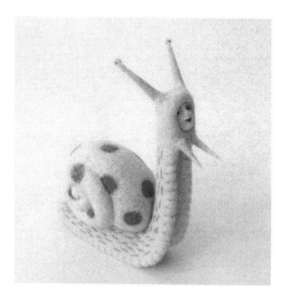

Oct. 3rd
In a boost to Chadwell's economy Microsoft has chosen to pump millions into Emily Potter's Haberdashery shop, Pumpkin Lane. The company will invest £106 million into the sewing retailer. A representative from Microsoft said 'we've seen the future – and the future is cotton reels.' 48,000 jobs will be created.

Oct. 4th
Don't forget the free concert at 1pm today in the Municipal Gardens! – where the Chadwell Salvation Army brass band will be playing hits from horror-punk combo The Screaming Dead, plus selections of psychobilly, garage hardcore & industrial death-metal. Tea & Biscuits included.

Oct. 5th
Good news, bad news. Bad news, Moffat's Clothing Factory Ltd. will be closing tomorrow with 1000 redundancies. Good news, the council will be offering every single employee the opportunity to retrain as a human cannonball. We're in this together. Text #Cannonball to 081495682.

Oct. 6th

My beloved citizens. Today I am posting images of the Battley Bunker, which I will be forced to inhabit in the event of nuclear attack. From this subterranean hell-hole, this ghastly cave, I shall monitor events until Chadwell is restored to glory. We're in this together. I love you.

Oct. 7th

Crazy times. John Craven opened our Rotary Fete today. Never again. He got completely p★★★ed on Mrs. Barlow's home-made wine & smashed the place up. Lifted the tombola aloft, screamed 'catch this, m'fers!' & hurled it at the Alderman's head. I'm never watching Countryfile again.

Oct. 8th

It is with heavy heart that I announce I've tested positive for apoplexy, biliousness & rickets. I'm being treated by our municipal apothecary, Silas Trevithick, who has prescribed being stroked across the temple with the leg of an unhappy ant, and & bowing hourly to a fig. Pray for me.

Oct. 9th
F★★★ing livid. Six months ago the council commissioned the building of a new Accounts Office from local architects Randall, Hopper & Nelson. This is the result. Very funny. Ha bloody ha. Does this scream Municipal Finance to you? I'll see you in court you acid-crazed b★★★★★ds.

Oct. 10th
Tomorrow I launch a brand new council initiative, 'Screen Free Saturday!' tackling kids' addiction to screens. Our programme will inform kids how we used to spend weekends. For example, a typical Saturday for me was Banana Splits, Laurel & Hardy, Flipper, Swapshop, Grandstand, Wrestling, Results, News, Weather with Bert Foord (yes, Foord), Top Cat, Pink Panther,

Dr. Who, Generation Game, Man From Uncle, Morecambe & Wise, Parky. We created our own fun! Kids have lost all that and need to have it drummed into them that we were much better than them.

Oct. 11th
Our hearts go out today to local man Alan Strang, who's been shielding inside a kitchen cabinet for 6 months. He emerged this morning in the belief it was all over, so our #CovidMarshalls immediately informed him of the second lockdown & stuffed him back in. Hang in there, Alan.

Oct. 12th

#JohnLennon80today. I met the lovely Fab Four when they played Chadwell Town Hall, '64. Afterwards we threw a reception for them, where I entertained them on the bassoon. As you can see they were thrilled, but for some reason I can't recall they suddenly made excuses and had to leave after 3 minutes. Happy days.

Oct. 13th

Ugly rumours are swirling that I plan to build on Chadwell's last remaining greenbelt. Let me be clear. As God is my witness, this beautiful landscape - admittedly small - will be protected for the enjoyment of citizens for centuries to come. WE WILL NEVER SELL THIS LAND!

Oct.14th

A fantastic evening of socially-distanced wrestling at Chadwell Baths! With no contact permitted, only psychic wrestlers are allowed to fight. Here Ted the Wizard levitates Kid Rampage for an astonishing six minutes to win the bout.

Oct. 16th

Frothing with rage. Once again the Dept. of Culture, Media & Sport refuse to grant Grade I listing to Chadwell's upside-down church. LOOK AT IT! IT'S AN UPSIDE DOWN CHURCH! What do you want from us – a sideways synagogue?! A tilted temple?!

I'm done with you.

Oct 18th

Great news! With couples now allowed to perform ballet, Mrs. Battley & I will be resuming our public dances in the open air theatre by the crazy golf course. Tomorrow, Swan Lake. And please – don't throw golf balls at us like last time. Have some respect.

Oct 19th
In an update on my medical condition I was airlifted today from my home in Battley Crescent to Chadwell Cottage Hospital. I only live next door, but nothing was left to chance. As you know I'm a battler, & I will fight this chronic wind with the forbearance of an Arthurian Knight.

Oct. 20th
Thrilled to announce that tonight I'm returning home from Chadwell Cottage Hospital. I feel great. Friends, do not let chronic wind dominate your life. I've been taking experimental drug Demoxifloxanimandrical. My eyebrows have fallen off but the flatulence is history. God bless.

Oct. 23rd
Delighted to meet the new Vicar of St. Chad's this evening over tea & Viennese Whirls at the vicarage. Cecil Trowbridge is a somewhat unconventional figure but I like the cut of his jib and his knowledge of Augustinian theodicy is second to none.

Oct. 24th
#SOCIAL DISTANCING. A gentle stroll along the canal towpath with my wife & children was utterly spoiled by someone walking straight towards us on the path and making no attempt to step aside. So I took matters into my own hands. I'm not proud of pushing a nun into the canal, but rules are rules.

Oct. 24th
Gutted. The fragile peace between flower & vegetable growers at Chadwell Allotments was shattered today when Alan Smith's pansies were set alight & Tina Brown's dwarf beans were mutilated & posted through her letterbox. I will arrange a meeting with the heads of the five families. This war stops now.

Oct. 25th
Every great leader must step up to the plate. Today I volunteered to trial an experimental treatment for Covid-19. I was stripped naked & lowered into a vat of kangaroo urine. We later discovered our medical officer is insane. But that didn't matter – the point is I stepped up.

Oct. 26th

As you know I swept to power on a manifesto of restoring not only the death penalty but also public executions. After a 5-year legal battle I've been told 'I'm not allowed to.' The above gallows, which I planned to restore to the town square, languishes in the local museum. A dark day.

Oct. 27th

Ok. Time to admit my scheme to reintegrate felons back into the community was a tad flawed. Giving work experience in a jewellers to three lifelong jewel thieves was, in hindsight, a decision that can best be described as 'rash.' As it happens they stole £20k & were last seen doing 90mph along the A39. But let's not play the blame game. Let's learn from this and move on.

Oct. 29th
#LOCKDOWN RULES.
So. My latest instructions on the lockdown are - and I quote -
'baffling,' are they? You cretins! Read my lips: BANNED:
Ping-Pong (but not after 6pm), Tai Chi, competitive knitting.
PERMITTED: Kung Fu, Cribbage, tap-dancing.
If that's not clear I wash my hands of the lot of you.

Oct. 30th
WE'RE HIRING! Chadwell Council is on the look out for a
new resident contortionist. Benefits include luncheon vouchers,
pension, and a velvet-lined suitcase to live in. Duties include
contorting between 9am-5pm. Must be able to fit in a drawer.
DM me.

Nov. 1st
FFS. Inbox rammed with complaints that I constantly 'nick
people's cars!' Excuse me?! Check the small-print in the bye-laws,
tw*ts! In the event of an emergency I am permitted to
commandeer ANY VEHICLE! Which is why tonight I drove to
Whist Club in Mr. Cottrell's Porsche. So do one.

Nov. 2nd
Yet again the Gazette accuses me of 'keeping Chadwell behind
the times.' Are they insane? Have they forgotten that Chadwell
boasts Britain's first openly bi-polar barber? A gay-friendly
Laser-Quest? The head of refuse-collection is a pansexual Inuit -
what more do you want?!

Nov. 3rd
A magnificent Annual Parade, in which Chadwell's three
Inter-Continental Ballistic Missiles rolled through the precinct.
Many critics have asked 'why does a small dormitory town in
South Northamptonshire possess intercontinental ballistic

missiles?' I simply say this. We are now ready to face anything Luton can throw at us.

Nov. 4th
MINUTES OF THE EXTRAORDINARY MEETING OF THE STEERING COMMITTEE 04/11/2020:
1. Apologies for absences.
2. No one here.
3. Meeting ends.
4. Ted Frost appears. Meeting resumes.
5. Ted suddenly remembers dentist's appointment, leaves.
6. Meeting ends.
I sometimes wonder why I bother.

Nov. 6th
Please vote in the upcoming election on Nov 3rd for Chairperson of the Park Bench Maintenance Committee. As you know my preferred candidate is Brenda Kaufman. Her opponent, Frank

Norton, has just been endorsed by the Taliban, which should tell you everything you need to know.

Nov. 7th
Good news, bad news. Today I declared Pott's Meadow a protected zone, owing to the presence of a rare great crested newt. Unfortunately during the press conference, I trod on the newt. The estate will now go ahead, and in honour of the creature will be named Reptile Boulevard.

Nov. 8th
I've just been informed by the Housing Committee that newts are not reptiles. The estate will therefore be named either Amphibian Gardens, or Lizard Crescent. This will go to a full vote of the council tomorrow. God bless.

Nov. 9th
#TIERSYSTEM
URGENT: Chadwell is largely spared the Governments' guidelines on tiers, with the exception of Mrs. Bunt of 32, Cowslip Lane. Her left leg has been declared a 'Tier-3' leg. Her limb will be closed down for 3 months, and she must hop everywhere. If you see her walking, arrest her.

Nov. 10th
When I was School Governor of St. Chadwells I was very proud of introducing a GCSE in Jousting. To my horror I'm told it may be dropped from the curriculum! Defeating an opponent on horseback with a lance is an essential life-skill. I've placed the school under special measures.

Nov. 13th
The council apologises for officially categorising the Chadwell Knitting Club as a terrorist organisation. We're looking into precisely how this happened - the net's closing on a former

member with a burning grudge. In short, Mrs. Lily Fox of Tip St. has some questions to answer.

Nov. 14th

Heads up. Tomorrow certain photos will appear in the press of me dancing in a nightclub in Ibiza with a girl called Nina. Let me be blunt. If two adults can't let their hair down after a heated conference on Municipal Finance then frankly I despair. Can we all grow up please?

Nov. 15th

There's no easy way to say this. Today the private data of every Chadwell resident was accidentally emailed to Vladimir Putin. Our IT supremo Colin Frost had one his turns, fell forward onto the keyboard & his head hit 'send.'
I'm pulling an all-nighter. We're on top of this.

Nov. 16th

As you know I'm Patron of Chadwell Locust Sanctuary, devoted to rehabilitating lost & bewildered locusts. Today we released 48,000, thinking they'd return to the wild. We were wrong. They terrorised the shopping centre & devoured 58 acres of nearby crops. For this we say sorry.

Nov. 17th

Well the Pub Quiz over Zoom was a f***ing catastrophe. Mrs. Mortlake fell asleep & slumped against her webcam the entire evening, and the Vicar got hammered on sherry & threw his glass at his laptop because he didn't know who played Colonel Pickering in My Fair Lady. Never again.

Nov. 18th

I believe in rehabilitation. Giving criminals a second chance. So today I took three prisoners on a trip to the Botanical Gardens. How did they repay my kindness? They knocked me out with a

mango, tied me to a breadfruit tree & fled. Rehabilitation my arse
– let the b★st★rds rot.

Nov. 19th
Every great leader struggles with hard choices. These past weeks I
agonised over spending £50,000 on an extension to the Drop-in
Centre, or commission an oil painting of myself. Then, like King
Solomon, I hit on a compromise: the painting will hang in the
Drop-in Centre! Namaste.

Nov. 20th

Myself & the FLOC - the First Lady of Chadwell - called President-Elect Biden's transition team earlier to offer our help to the new administration. For security reasons they spoke in code - 'Who is this? Go away.' What they clearly meant was 'thank you, great suggestion, we admire you.'

And so to my volunteer work. For my stint on Chadwell Hospital Radio this evening I booked an 'easy-listening middle-of-the-road artiste.' Who do they send?- Industrial Thrash-Metal singer Sex Watson. He's halfway through 'Death is my Middle Name.' 6 patients have discharged themselves. God help us all.

Nov. 21st
I take my sport uber seriously, so today I took my team out on a ruthless fitness programme. Nina Bunt (87) ran 15 miles & swam 600m in icy water: & Ted Fosset (76) did 100 push-ups & walked across burning coals. I'll build the best Shove Ha'penny team in the West Fens or perish in the attempt.

Nov. 22nd
There's a 2-for-1 deal on Attercliffe's Faggots & Peas at Mace's store on Thrust Street. In the interests of full disclosure I've been paid £150,000 to make this announcement.

That can't be right. I've just checked Sid's email and I'm pretty sure he must have meant £15.00. He can't type at the best of times – in fact no one's ever seen him without his arthritis gloves on. I won't hold him to it.

Nov. 24th

Jesus wept. Yet again the Chadwell Sunday Bugle is running a story on the 'dubious state of my finances.' WTAF? Yes this is my villa in Mustique – deal with it! May I remind you who restored law & order to Chadwell by smashing the lollipop ladies strike of 2008? You sicken me.

Nov. 25th

It's been a tough time for local businesses so I'm overjoyed to see green shoots of recovery sprouting across our beloved town. I am thrilled to announce the re-opening of Chadwell's famous Waxwork Museum, Judd St., Tues–Sun 10-6. (Formerly Hooper's Shop-window Mannequins Ltd.).

Sad news. I met Diego Maradonna in 1992 when he was on a sketching tour of Bedfordshire. We had a lovely chat in the snug bar of the Grouse & Goose, Dunstable. Lovely chap, but for someone so good with his hands he was lamentable at shove ha-penny. I beat him 11-0. RIP.

Nov. 26th
And so the elections loom for Chairperson of Parish Bridleways &
Footpaths. As ever I remain utterly impartial. I shall just say this
about candidate Frank Simmons.
Look at him.
Everything about him screams 'Putin's puppet.'

Nov. 27th
Delivering a talk tonight at the Rotary Cub on my Grandfather,
Shadrack Battley. An intelligence officer in WW1, he penetrated
enemy lines disguised as a pork chop. Tragically he was captured
in Vienna and turned into schnitzel. Awarded a posthumous
George Cross. To Shadrack!

Nov. 28th
FFS. Like many great leaders I've set up an emergency escape plan,
like in Line of Duty. Today I sat on my mobile & accidentally
triggered it. The Crump twins appeared with shotguns & whisked

me off in a souped-up Cortina. We were on the A1 before I could abort. Still trembling.

Nov. 29th
Holy Moly. I've discovered the insurance value of all Chadwell's buildings is £850 million. With a population of 10,000 that's 85 grand each! Meaning we could demolish the town tonight & split the dosh! Just a thought. I'll leave it with you.

Nov. 30th
Good news, bad news. Good news, we've completed our Shoreline Management Plan, costing £2 million, outlining Chadwell's coastal defences against erosion. Bad news, we've just realised we're 60 miles from the coast. But hey, life's a learning curve! Let's laugh at this & move on.

Dec. 1st
As you know I'm a recent convert to an offshoot of mindfulness - hatfulness: the wearing of different headpieces to cultivate well-being. A top hat for confidence, bowler for efficiency, panama trilby for relaxation etc. Today I am wearing a bonnet to emphasise my feminine side.

Dec. 2nd
FFS. Deluged with complaints that my Support Package during the circuit-break lockdown is, and I quote, 'pitiful b★l★ks! Excuse me? A parcel containing a Twix, a sachet of Ovaltine & a copy of my volume of poetry, & you dare to denounce this as insufficient? I'm on the verge of resigning.

Dec. 3rd
Rejoice! Our pilot scheme of 'overhead pedestrian wires' is a resounding success, saving us millions in pedestrianisation. Only three people plunged to the ground, a statistic I am willing to live with. Tight-rope lessons are available in the drop-in centre 12–2pm.

Dec. 4th
Catastrophe. Laid up in Chadwell General with multiple sporting injuries. I suppose I've only myself to blame - I've always given

110% in everything I do. Niggling feeling it's time I admitted shove ha-penny's a young man's game.

Dec. 5th

It is with a deep sense of shame that yesterday, after a drunken night in the Railway Tavern, I appointed this chicken Deputy Mayor. In the cold light of day this struck me as foolhardy. I can categorically state that this morning the bantam has been stripped of all its administrative powers.

Dec. 8th
Lovely couple over for dinner, the Musgroves. He's a doctor and she's a surgeon. What I like about them is that they don't mind talking shop. He was very helpful in advising my wife on her frozen shoulder & between courses Mrs. Musgrove operated on my gallstones. A happy evening.

Dec. 9th
As a lifelong nudist I derive succour from rolling naked in moss. This is best done in remote woodland, far from prying eyes. It is not ideal when done in one's front garden. Which is why I was arrested this morning. I'd like to apologise to the passing milkman, who threw two pints of gold top into the air and ran away screaming.

Dec. 10th

Thrilled to announce I've just approved a space centre to be built next to ASDA. The Battley Wonder-Thrust will launch in 2025 and land on the outer ring of the Battley Crater, Mars. My DNA will then be used to populate the Red Planet, creating a world of councillors. At least that's the plan.

Rejoice!

Dec. 11th

One of the darkest days in Chadwell's history was the Great Hat Shortage of 1922. Rivalling the horrific bowler-drought of 1890, naked heads were the norm. When a beret was spotted in the High St., gang-fights broke out. 16 died fighting over a cap. But we pulled through. #HatDay

Dec. 16th

Only a few tickets left for my seminar on leadership, Be Like Me or Fail, at the Mr. Pastry Conference Centre tomorrow 2pm–4pm. I tell my own story of how I overcame chilblains to become the most famous councillor in South Norhamptonshire. For £7.50, share a slice of my greatness.

★

MISSING - FIELD! Meadow theft is on the rise. Two pastures were stolen last week and a paddock vanished yesterday. I did not become a councillor to stand by and watch greenswards purloined under our noses. If you see this field being sold in a Cash-Converter, call 0800754611.

Dec. 17th
PARISH NOTICE: In spite of the hurricane, today's origami-themed picnic on Porlock Hill WILL take place. Repeat, WILL take place. Remember to bring lots of crepe-paper for the paper-hat contest.

Dec. 18th

A sad day. Just back from the funeral of Bill Prentice, who served Chadwell loyally for 50 yrs as head of traffic management. In accordance with his wishes he was melted down & made into a traffic-cone, which now stands in the park.

God bless you, Bill.

Cone, but not forgotten.

Dec. 19th
As a youth I was a devout Hindu, and at times of difficulty like now I still turn to the wisdom of my former guru, Maharishi Swami Prabavanda Surumiyatta Gopal. His real name was Alan Enstridge and he worked in a garden centre in Tring. But that didn't matter – cosmic wisdom is cosmic wisdom.

2021

Jan.. 3rd
Good news, bad news. Bad news, the number of people allowed at a wedding has been reduced to one. Good news, the vicar's reporting a boom in solo weddings. Bob Carter at St. Chad's earlier today, getting married to himself. Good luck, Bob.

Jan. 8th
Off to a book launch! – Miles Green's monumental history of our town, 'Chadwell – the First 15 Billion Years.' 400 pages are devoted to the formation of the galaxy when Chadwell was stardust. Sadly Miles can't be there – he's now a patient in Sunnylawns Asylum. But we wish him well.

Jan. 11th
Raging. The Tourist Board has stripped Chadwell Model Village of its license. Bastards! True, it's not strictly a model village – tourists are taken to a nearby hill and shown the actual Chadwell from a distance. It was a big money-maker for the town for decades. I will appeal.

Jan. 12th
Grave news. We strongly believe Russia was behind a massive cyber-attack today on the council's mainframe, and the answer to the Guess the Number of Jellybeans contest in the town hall foyer stolen. We're battling to install a firewall.
Meanwhile we've added jellybeans to the jar. We will not be cowed by Putin.

Jan. 13th
Thrilled that my scout troop, the First Chadwell Eagles, have returned from their successful undercover mission to Russia, where they monitored military installations along the Ukranian border. Tonight I awarded them their 'Enemy Infiltration' badges. Next stop North Korea!

Jan. 20th
Six weeks ago Chadwell Council bought 14 million doses of the #Pfizervaccine. Owing to some ghastly clerical error we administered all the doses to Colin Potter of 32, Abbattoir Gdns. Good news: he's stable. Bad news: he's the size of a hot-air balloon.
I have two simple words. Those two words are: sorry Colin.

Jan. 25th
I can now reveal that for many months I have been working on a Covid-19 vaccine in my kitchen. Six weeks ago I sent the results

of my findings to #Pfizer. Clearly they were impressed by my fusion of crushed moth wings and Bovril. I'm certainly not claiming sole credit. But we all played our part.

Jan. 26th
Thrilled to unveil the prototype of Chadwell's new council house. 2,000 of these 'shoe cottages' will be rolled out across the borough from 2023. They will be available to all, but priority will be given to women with so many children they don't know what to do.

Jan. 27th
FFS. Earlier today I declared a state of emergency. I was told a wild animal was on the loose & had killed 23 people. I called the army in.
This is that animal.
Ok. Listen up, m'fers. One more prank call like that and you're going down.
The State of Emergency is over.

Jan. 28th
After agonising delays Margaret Nuttall has finally been elected Deputy Footpath Officer. She says her aim is to 'heal division, spread light where once there was darkness, revitalise the national economy and vanquish hatred with humanity.' Slightly ambitious when you're only in charge of bridle-paths, but congrats anyway.

Jan. 30th
Sadly Chadwell's Annual Running of the Minks will not take place tomorrow. As you know, like the bulls in Pamplona, 100,000 mink are released into the town, chasing us down the High St., crawling over us and biting as we laugh with joy. After much agonising debate, this is cancelled.

Feb 10th
I love #WorldKindnessDay, a permanent fixture of Chadwell's calendar. It's a day when our citizens go out of their way to perform little acts of love & respect. Today I'm being carried everywhere in a sedan chair by four old age pensioners. My heart is bursting with love.
Feb 15th

FFS! Once again my day has been destroyed. So looking forward to the match tonight. Frank's pulled a calf muscle, Cecil's on a red card, and Marjory's cried off with groin strain. I'll have to play my Second Team. We were so close to that Dominoes gold cup we could smell it!

Feb 19th
When I swept to power the first thing on my to-do list was to ensure my beloved Cecil roamed freely in the town hall. Of course the killjoys said 'what the f★★★s a leopard doing in the council chamber?' – but he's now loved by all, and has hardly bitten anyone.

March 1st
I give up. Alan Randall's wedged in the alleyway again between Hope Street and the precinct. How many more times? The f★★★ing thing's impassable! Sixteen people have got stuck in it since the bloody thing was built. It's 6 inches wide! Read my lips: If you want to get to to the High Street WALK AROUND SODDING BETFRED!

March 9th
Thrilled! I am finally to be inducted into the Councillor Hall of
Fame! Scandalously, I've been overlooked for years, but luckily in
2020 I find myself head of the selection committee. Of course
one must be impartial, but thankfully I am objectively the best, so
voted for myself.

★

March 12th
Simmering with fury. I'm accused of breaching the Councillor's Code of Conduct! WTAF? If a man can't throw a fellow Councillor out of a 3rd-floor window I don't want to live in Britain any more. He fell into a skip full of mattresses! Not my fault he bounced & landed in the canal. I will appeal.

March 19th
Update on last month's fiasco when owing to a glitch in the council's payroll software, lollipop lady Fran Cottrell was paid £14 million. We've tracked her down to her villa in Tuscany and are in contact with her butler. We're working tirelessly with the Italian Government on an extradition order.

April 8th
Not a good day. Timmy Mallett, while gracious enough to open Chadwell's new arboretum, got completely hammered and urinated in a yukka. And that's not all. He then attacked a breadfruit tree, screaming 'I'll take you all on, you wooden m'fers!' You think you know someone.

April 16th
Last week I wrote to the Prime Minister requesting that Mrs. Battley be declared an Area of Outstanding Natural Beauty. His reply was curt & dismissive. I've since discovered that I do have power over public spaces, so I hereby announce that my wife is now a park. No trespassing is allowed obviously but you are free to enjoy her beauty. Just study your byelaws.

April 21st
Like many great leaders I am a disciple of Machiavelli, and strive each day to put his theories into practice. Some might say that implementing measures originating in medieval Italy is "old-fashioned." I beg to differ. So today I banished Colin Potter

from Chadwell on pain of death and sentenced him to live in exile in Luton.

April 12th
I'd like to thank landscape gardener Reg Potter and his assistants Darryl & Monty for doing a wonderful job in transforming the industrial wasteland on the edge of town into this lovely vista. Looking at these before & after pics, hard to believe they achieved this in a weekend.

April 23rd
Beginning to regret introducing Dress-up Friday at the Town Hall. This is Carol Hargreaves and Nigel Mottram of the Ways & Means Committee deep in discussion on the extension to the ring-road.

April 25th
Crunch talks on the proposed alleyway between Micky Rooney Lane & Beethoven St. - slashing pedestrian journey times to the precinct by 30 seconds - reach their #endgame. If discussions break down it will set Chadwell back 1000 years. I can't lie and say I haven't taken a valium.

May 3rd
Can I nip this in the bud please? Read my lips: I am NOT putting Chadwell through a #GreatReset. This is NOT an on-off button that will restore the town to its 1965 settings - it's a drainage

cover in Farmer Porlock's upper meadow. Can we just get a grip? You sicken me.

May 9th
Quite right too. I'm fully behind Ted at the Maudlin Trumpet.
My blood runs cold when I recall the night those Morris dancing
savages from Kettering set upon the Chadwell Shove-Ha'penny
League and thrashed them with their sticks. THE

BAN REMAINS! If I see one gartered sock anywhere in this
municipality you'll be tasered.

May 15th

May 15th

It's all go down at the Drop-in Centre as we gear up for a Eurovision party to end all Eurovision parties! The Ferguson 16" TV is warming up and Ron Bonce has made some of his special broth. It's going to be crazee-ee-ee-ee!

May 14th
#DININGRESTRICTIONS
Disturbing scenes outside the Anne Boleyn Tea-rooms this lunchtime. I've imposed martial law. Read my lips: ONE TOASTED TEACAKE PER PERSON, plus one rectangle of individual foil-wrapped Anchor butter. Anyone ordering Welsh Rarebit will be shot.

June 1st
I speak on behalf of Chadwell's thriving mouse community. Can we *please* be mindful of our cats when strolling through the town's Mouse Quarter? Mice retail has suffered enough from the lockdowns – in fact I'm meeting the Mouse Alderman today to outline the support package.

June 4th
Chadwell FC would like to apologise for tonight's utter fiasco of a football match. It transpires that they invited a crowd, but forgot to invite the teams. They've asked me to pass on the following message: 'We feel such fools. We got it the wrong way round. Many apologies.'

June 5th
Every great leader is plagued by the 'black dog' of melancholy. Following the reduction in the Footpath Maintenance Budget today I have plunged into a slough of despond equal to King Lear's. Typing this from beneath a pile of blankets in my shed. I will not emerge until tomorrow.

June 8th
A great day in the history of Chadwell. The famous artist Banksy has created this wonderful work of art on the side of the public conveniences in the Municipal Gardens. Now valued at £18 million, the building will be turned into a Museum. Rejoice!

June 15th
Rumours are circulating that the council is using a remote-controlled white balloon - a 'Rover' - to stop people from leaving Chadwell. What kind of psychotic monsters do you take us for? It's only an experiment. If you don't like it we'll drop it. Sheesh, calm down.

June 20th

#SOCIALDISTANCING Ok. Last night I attended a funeral wake at the British Legion for dear old Lanky Musgrove, ex-bugler for the Chadwell First Yeomanry. Things got out of hand and I ended up diving into a mosh-pit to the strains of Vera Lynn. It was a momentary lapse. Let's laugh & move on.

June 21st

#SCHOOLL OCKDOWN I give up. Spent four hours today teaching my son Pericles Maths & English, only to discover he'd replaced himself with a ventriloquist's dummy & sneaked out into the garden. Can I afford to waste my time home-schooling puppets?! THERE ARE BELISHA BEACONS CRYING OUT TO BE FIXED!

July 1st
Rigid with anger. Today I called the Dept. of Health proposing
the use of Octopuses to #vaccinate people, as they could do 8 in
one go. Matt Hancock swears at me and slams the 'phone down.
WTAF?! All week I've been training an octopus to hold a
hypodermic. Waste of f★★★king time.

July 7th
Proud to say St. Chadwell's is the only church in Britain where
vegetables & fruit are permitted to marry. This is Bob & Tina
who tied the knot yesterday. They are currently honeymooning
in the allotments. Next week we will be blessed with the nuptials
of a radish and a fig.

July 14th
Yesterday I informed the Mayor of Uttoxeter that if he hadn't withdrawn his scout-troop from Chadwell Park by 11o'clock, then a state of war would exist between us. I have to tell you now, that no such assurance has been received, and that consequently we are at war with Uttoxeter.

July 15th
Inspired by the PM's merger of Difid and the Foreign Office, today I will merge Chadwell's Head of Open Spaces with the Waste Management Chief, to form the Head of Wasted Space.

July 19th
Your ignorance makes me pulsate with rage. Who in their right mind would think I'd reduced social distancing to a compulsory 1 millimetre? Are you brain-dead?! It's one METRE! This is a group of people today in the park. We had to prise them apart with crowbars. Off to whist.

July 20th
To mark the 10th anniversary of the Chadwell Naturist Society, at 6pm this evening I will be drifting naked down the canal on a lilo, accompanied by my fellow nudists. All except Mrs. Brunswick, whose sciatica is playing up something rotten. Enjoy!

July 21st
Lockdown easing taking effect. My cousin Ken and his wife Donna drove over from Uttoxeter today for a socially-distanced visit. Haven't seen them for months. As it happens we hate them so we hid behind the sofa & pretended to be out. But it was nice they had the opportunity.

July 24th
Disaster. Cooked Mrs. Battley a meal tonight of seared bream with wilted spinach basted with squid ink. Forgot to buy squid ink so used contents of fountain pen. For the last twenty minutes she's been projectile vomiting like a stunt double in the Exorcist. And so to Evensong.

July 26th
Simmering with fury. Several 'do-gooders,' (tw*ts) have outed me as breaking lockdown by regularly visiting Fat Ron's Guzzle Shack on the bypass. HE'S MY SUPPORT BUBBLE YOU MORONS! WHERE ELSE AM I GOING TO GET MY DAILY SAUSAGE FRITTER?!
And so to prayers.

July 27th

Very nostalgic for #Glastonbury tonight. In 1976 myself & the future Mrs. Battley loaded up our pink VW camper van and headed south. Wild, wild days. This is me dancing to The Carpenters. Hard to believe that a fortnight later I was elected Deputy Chairman of the Ways & Means Committee.

July 28th

URGENT: Incidents of 'dogging' in Chadwell have increased by 250% in the last twelve weeks. This Bacchanalian frenzy is getting out of hand. I take this very very seriously - which is why I have

personally been monitoring the lay-by near Fossett Wood every
night for three months.

July 29th
Well the interfaith barbecue in the Municipal Gardens was an
almighty cluster-f**k. Massive punch-up between the
Episcopalians and the Jainists, and a nun went nuts with a spatula.
One thing I've taken away from the whole ghastly experience –
never throw a lamb chop at a Druid.

July 30th
Makes me laugh, politicians constantly needing to prove their
physical fitness. Fit? Fit? The electorate of Chadwell know I make
Arnold Schwarzenegger look like Charles Hawtrey. Myself and
Mrs. Battley earlier today –

August 1st
Tonight I flew to London on my Learjet, Councillor 1, for crisis
talks with the Prime Minister. He was out. I left a note, had a

light supper in Wagamamas, and flew back. Further updates to follow.

August 2nd

My local business of the week award goes to Bing Shropshire, who has been selling his jugs of tea in the Municipal Gardens for 45 years. 'The odd thing is,' confessed Bing, 64, 'is that I don't even like tea. I hate it. And I hate people.' We wish him many more years of success.

August 3rd
Our 'Bring a Deer to Work Day' passes off admirably. Here, Parks Supremo Colin Thorneycroft studies flowerbed design while being stared at by an antelope. An update on Bob Laidlaw who was gored by a rutting reindeer in the tea-room – he's stable and off the danger-list.

August 7th
As Chairman of Chadwell FC it is with heavy heart that I announce we've had to let Jimmy 'Goalmouth' Bradstock go. Frankly, this last season he's been a huge disappointment: his speed, stamina and ball-skills have been rubbish. Besides, at 93 it's about time he hung up his boots.

Aug. 4th
I'm a committed environmentalist. I love environments. My reforestation campaign has been a triumph. But we need to do more. We must grow trees *inside* our houses. You heard me. I want sycamores in everyone's living-rooms. Poplars in bathrooms. Oaks in lean-to's. We can do this!!

Sept. 12th
URGENT: Can I please urge all residents to obey planning permission rules? Too often our beloved town is blighted by houses that simply don't fit in. Take my house, for example – Battley Grange. I wanted it 100 ft high and with a moat, but I thought no, keep it simple. Rant over.

Sept. 23rd
Ok. Listen up. This NOT a vigilante zombie. This is Ted Stubbs, your cheery Covid-friendly milkman, doing his rounds clad in PPE. So stop attacking him. Yesterday he was chased down the road by children & pelted with apples. He dropped two pints of gold-top. Leave him alone!

Oct. 4th

Ok. Has a mysterious giant zip been spotted on the borders of our town? Yes. Does this mean Chadwell is attached to Britain with a YKK fastener & the council are planning to unzip the town and move to the Italian Riviera? Possibly. Be assured, we are only at the DISCUSSION stage.

Oct. 26th

Delighted to be speaking at the #COP26 summit in Glasgow. To be exact I'm chairing a fringe meeting next door in the snug bar of the Thistle & Codpiece. To ensure that Chadwell leads the way in reducing our carbon footprint, I can announce that we ARE BANNING SPAGHETTI CARBONARA.

Oct. 30th

With heavy heart I announce the closure of Chadwell Petting Zoo. Six deaths a month in a place where the biggest animals are rabbits is frankly unacceptable. This is all that remains of Mr. Albert Christ as he stopped for a picnic in the dormouse enclosure. It ends now.

Nov. 2nd

A dark day. My attempt to extend my emergency powers to include executions is roundly rejected. Surely the ability to eliminate people is a valuable tool in any Parish Councillor's arsenal? I wasn't *insisting* on the guillotine! I merely suggested it. Sheesh. And so to Evensong.

Nov. 4th
Ok. Can we all calm down please? Thank you.
Some answers.
Did I order 40,000 duck masks by mistake as PPE for Chadwell Cottage Hospital?

Yes.

Is this Doctor Frank Cottrell?

Yes.

Does he mind wearing a duck mask?

No.

Now - can we ple-ease just relax and enjoy our evenings? FFS.

Nov.9th

Look. We all have bad days. But I will not have Chadwell's traffic-lights subjected to such appalling disregard. I have written to the person responsible, informing him in no uncertain terms that this is not the behaviour we expect from an archbishop.

Nov. 11th

Proud to say that today I was vaccinated at Chadwell Cottage Hospital! I had the Melton Mowbray vaccine. Absolutely no side-effects whatsoever, apart from a thin veneer of short-crust pastry covering me from head to foot, and the sudden appearance of an egg in my inside pocket.

Nov. 14th
WHOAH! The Chadwell WW2 Re-enactment Society, whose aim is to re-enact the entire Second World War from start to finish, are getting out of hand. Today they reduced Kwiksave to rubble and the manager of Spud-U-Like is in a POW camp near the bypass. STOP IT!

Nov. 15th
It is with heavy heart that I must announce that an epidemic of cocaine-fuelled parties have been sweeping our beloved town. I can now reveal that over the last 3 months I have gone undercover & attended 63 of these vile events. My research is not yet complete. I'll report back.

Nov. 16th
UPDATE: Professor Nuttall's lecture last night in the Town Hall, entitled 'Is Cannibalism ALWAYS wrong?' was cancelled today, following a police raid and seizure of 120 sausages-on-sticks. I'm still reeling, but make no mistake Nuttall's days as a leading Rotary Club member are numbered.

Nov. 19th
When I took office in 1997 I made it perfectly clear that Kettering should never be allowed to acquire a nuclear weapon. Tonight I've been informed that an enriched uranium facility has been spotted in woods off the A14. We are therefore at war with Kettering. We attack tomorrow.

Nov. 21st

I like to keep up morale in the town hall. Today it was 'Bring Your Bees & Clarinet to Work' day. Here Mr. Fothergill from accounts entertains us with Gershwin's Rhapsody in Blue while cloaked in his happy swarm.

Dec. 1st

For many years I've been raising awareness of the plight of homeless lizards. Every Christmas the citizens of Chadwell throw open their doors to Bearded Dragons, newts and other reptiles down on their luck. They are fed, clothed, and given a bed for the Christmas period. If you want to register, please email iwantalizard@chadwellcouncil.co.uk

Dec. 2nd
Mrs. Battley's Christmas single drops tonight. She's fused
Louisiana swamp-pop with Latvian death-funk in the most daring
arrangement of 'I'm a Little Teapot Short and Stout' ever released.
It premieres tonight at 4am on my Chadwell Hospital Radio slot,
Bop With Battley. #ChristmasNo1

Dec. 15th
The Archbishop of Chadwell arriving at St. Brenda's to deliver his
Christmas message. Niggling feeling he may have gone slightly
over the top with the PPE, but hey ho. We think he read from
Ecclesiastes, but to be honest no one could hear a word he was
saying.

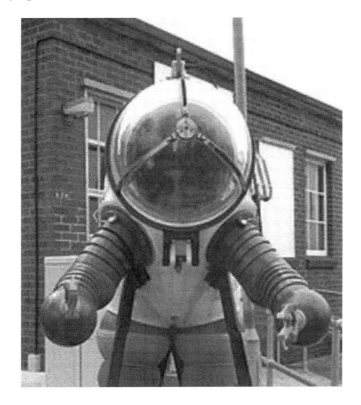

Dec.16th

I applaud Boris Johnson's declaration that Britain remains culturally, emotionally & geologically connected with Europe. I know exactly what he means – in 1976 Chadwell District council separated from Stevenage Borough Council, but we remain culturally, emotionally and sexually connected.

Dec. 17th

I rarely compare myself to Christ. I leave that to others. But each year I trudge the snowy streets of Chadwell and deliver a gift to all of my beloved citizens. This is me last night on my lonely vigil. A Merry Christmas to all my people! But not if you moved here from Luton.

Dec. 18th

Incandescent with rage. Last month I signed off £100,000 for a 'Christmas display to equal Trafalgar Square.' And we end up with this. I am in urgent contact with my Head of Open Spaces, Spatchcock O'Shaughnessy, who apparently has done a runner to the Caribbean. Heads will roll.

Dec.19th

I have just got off the 'phone to EU Commissioner Barnier & Prime Minister Johnson, congratulating them on the #BrexitDeal. Mischievous as ever, they pretended not to know me, the scallywags. Ha ha. I assured them of Chadwell's full support as we forge ahead. And so to Evensong.

★

Dec. 20th

There's nothing that says Christmas more to me & Mrs. Battley than aluminium. Here we are, next to our aluminium tree on our very first Christmas at Battley Grange. Every Christmas Eve we stand to attention for 2 hours, then, clutching our copy of The Joy of Sex, we run upstairs.

Dec. 21st
My annual Santa-bunjee-jump over the River Chad, seconds before the line broke. Things are a bit hazy - I'm currently on

heavy medication - but I'd like to thank the owners of the passing tug-boat, the Saucy Minx. Merry Christmas everyone. Atchoo! Sorry, don't why I typed that.

Dec. 22nd
You utter bs'tds. For the third year in a row the giant inflatable snowman in my front garden has been shot with an airgun. I DEMAND RESPECT! PC Logan & myself will be on all-night stake-out tonight - if so much as one bauble is shattered with a pea-shooter, you're going down.

Dec. 25th
Every Christmas Day the Chadwell Nudists go for a festive swim in the icy River Bilberry. This year we're all wearing PPE - but be assured, underneath that diving-suit I'm completely and utterly naked. Merry Christmas!

2022

Jan. 2nd
It is with great sadness I announce the retirement of Lady Cecilia
Harcourt Babberly-Swinnerton, who served the council well for
more than fifty years. She will be sorely missed. Hand on heart, in
all honesty, I can say that she was one of the council's finest refuse
collectors.

Jan. 11th
Good news, bad news. Good news, we've completed our Shoreline Management Plan, costing £2 million, outlining Chadwell's coastal defences against erosion. Bad news, we've just realised we're 60 miles from the coast. But hey, life's a learning curve! Let's laugh at this & move on.

Jan.15th
WTAF?! I've been informed by my lawyer Hieronymous Cork that there's a deepfake tik-tok doing the rounds of me wrestling a kangaroo. Does anyone in their right mind think it's actually me?! I've got better things to do than engage in fisticuffs with a marsupial, I'VE A RING-ROAD TO PLAN!

Jan. 19th
There's no easy way to say this, but Mrs. Battley has knitted a blanket for a field. She's also knitting scarves for trees and giant beanie-hats for hills. Quite frankly I fear for her sanity. I foresee a day when the entire town of Chadwell is encased in wool. This can't go on.

Jan. 20th
Today is the 90th anniversary of the explosion of the Flump factory, when Chadwell was buried under a marshmallow mountain. The citizens were rescued by Bob Harbottle, who heroically ate his way out. On his tomb are the words – 'He sacrificed his waistline for the town he loved.'

Jan. 21st

A great day! At long last the statue of Mrs. Battley was unveiled in the park. Usual protesters shouting 'WTF did that cost?' etc., but otherwise a happy day.

(NB. On your council tax bills from now on you will see:

Police

Education

Re-cycling

Statue fund.

Pay it with pride.)XX

Jan 25th
Ok. Rumours are swirling that I have my own 'Q,' an inventor of secret weapons. Let me be clear. Do I have a biro that fires a laser-beam? Yes. Do I have a missile-launching traffic-cone & a jet-pack? Yes. The truth is, Sleaford could invade any minute. YOU CAN'T HANDLE THE TRUTH!

Jan. 30th
Ok. Here we go again. I didn't spend 10 yrs making Chadwell the erotic capital of Northants to have it smashed by Covid. I will never apologise for classifying Chadwell's sex shops as essential retail, and that includes Madam Beazley's Cave of Delights and World of Rumpy-Pumpy on the bypass.

Feb. 14th
Don't get me wrong. I'm ecstatic at the success of #MarsPerseverance. But we can PLEASE have some publicity about Chadwell's own council-run space-station, the Battley IV? This is Barabbas Cork on a space-walk. Tomorrow he will hold what is believed to be first ever Fete in space.

Feb. 18th
All my life I've fought for equality. I'm proud to say we have a female Education Secretary, female Head of Recycling, female Health & Safety Officer, & a female park-keeper. Admittedly it's all the same woman - Nina Potts. Great girl. Gets a bit tired but she's bloody versatile.

March 1st
I would like to address the rumours that I have built myself a private castle overlooking the town. My response to this accusation is simple, honest & direct. Yes. Now can we ple-ease move on to more important matters? We're trying to tackle a pandemic here!! Have a good evening.

March 3rd
The council apologises on behalf of Ted Padstow for firing at three Messerchmitts during today's flypast over Chadwell. He claims he 'had a flashback to 1940,' - a trifle puzzling as he was born in 1963. Quite why he has an M270B1 anti-aircraft gun in his back garden is not known.

March 11th
I see. It's like that, is it? It's acceptable to graffiti 'Battley is a w***er' on the side of the Co-op? Fine! Well let me tell you something, m'fers. I have six Chieftan tanks primed and ready to go. Any more mockery and I WILL DESTROY YOU!

March 17th
The council is debating whether to change the name of the road between the bowling green and the bottle-bank from 'Death Comes to Us All Street,' to 'Maple Crescent.' No idea why it has that grisly name. We suspect the road-naming officer, Barry Twist, was depressed at the time.

March 18th

When my son Pericles set off for school this morning in his Moby Dick costume for #WorldBookDay, I'm not ashamed to say I brushed away a municipal tear. Imagine my pride, then, upon hearing he has won First Prize at St. Tina's Mixed Infants. #ProudFather! #ProudCouncillor!

March 21ST

Remembering my beloved Father, Marmaduke Battley, 1920-2006. From the picture you'd think he was a Mayor, but actually he just liked dressing up as one. Diagnosed with Mayorphrenia, the delusion that you're a councillor, he ended his days in Chadwell Asylum, governing a flowerbed.

March 25th

Chadwell Zoo re-opens on the 12th! I'd like to thank everyone who gave a foster home to the animals during lockdown, particularly Mr. Bunt who took in 5 giraffes and a whale. Special thanks also to the Robinsons who had a gorilla in their granny-flat until the unfortunate incident.

April 5th
You sicken me. This is Rodney Farrell, our entertainments officer. All day he's been wandering Chadwell dressed as the Easter Bunny handing out eggs to children & old folk. This photo was taken seconds before he was thrown in the canal. Are you proud of yourselves? WELL ARE YOU?!

April 14th
I can't take any more. Reg in procurement orders 15 new refuse lorries, and what arrives? Dinky toys. What the hell are we going to collect in that - bloody microbes?! I know Ron the driver's small but even he'd struggle to squeeze into that. I'm off to the Lamb & Crumpet.

April 18th
I'd like thank the cast of BBC's Repair Shop for the fantastic job they've done on Chadwell Town Hall! Before & after pics below. We thought they'd just give it a lick of paint, maybe bit of re-pointing, but – well, look for yourselves. Our episode goes out in May. #RepairShop

April 19th
Just completed a random drugs test of all council staff. Shocked that one employee has tested positive for Horse, Ket, Meow-Meow, Charlie Whizz, White Lightning, Bombay Blue & Purple Hearts. A crying shame. Tabitha Dalrymple has served us well as a lollipop lady for more than 60 years.

April 21st
Ok. People are complaining that the new speed-bump on Pottery Boulevard is a tad on the high side. True, Barry Stipend in traffic control got centimetres mixed up with feet - we've all done it - but personally I can't see anything wrong with it. It stays.
Swivel, snowflakes.

April 23rd
Well someone's broken lockdown. Went to feed cat this evening
- nowhere to be found. Searched neighbourhood - found him off
his head in the snug bar of the Lucky Crumpet. Carrying him
back home now as he sings bawdy songs.

April 24th
Apoplectic with fury! Dept. of Health are closing down Chadwell
Industrial Estate! For 100 years we've been the biggest producer
of asbestos in Europe, and wear that badge with pride. Suddenly,
there's 'something wrong with asbestos.' WELL SORRY FOR
TRYING TO MAKE A LIVING!

April 25th
Rigid with shame. Police are hunting members of the Chadwell
Jane Austen Society, who were involved in a punch-up last night
with the Dickens Club outside the Surly Goose. Any info call

0800 431694. Do NOT approach – they are extremely dangerous and armed with silk gloves and snuff-boxes.

April 27th
Not again. Mr. Fothergill's Komodo Dragon has escaped. It was last seen browsing the Findus Crispy Pancakes in Londis after trying on all the dresses in Dorothy Perkins. EVERYBODY IN!

UPDATE. After breaking into Majestic Wines he drank 50 bottles of Valpolicella and is now sleeping it off in the allotments, where Gus Enstridge has wrapped him in heavy-duty gooseberry netting. Panic over.

April 29th
Today I will be fusing the Department of Waste Management with the Department of Time & Motion to create a department of Wasted Time. Happy Easter.

April 30th
Chadwell Easter Fete gets off with a bang. Bad news – the Antiquarian Society's demonstration of a medieval rack resulted in Stumpy Ron Mackenzie (4ft 6) being stretched to 6ft 4. Good news – at least he's now been picked for the Chadwell Basketball team. And so to the beer tent.

The Fete is passing off nicely, bar a few wrinkles. In hindsight, placing the Bash the Rat stall next to the display of pet rodents was a tad reckless. Latest reports are 3 concussed hamsters, 2 gerbils in intensive care & a guinea pig with advanced delirium tremens.

May 1st
Catastrophe. Bank Holiday carnage! This is our beloved precinct earlier today – water-mains burst, cars overturned, shops destroyed. Surely a question-mark is hovering over our annual Running of the Weasel.

May 11th
Good luck to Chadwell FC in their match tomorrow. We're having a tough season so far, and it's a crying shame that owing to an administrative error we've been drawn against Brazil. A tad worrying, as Nobby Padstow's just had a double hip replacement. Do Chadwell proud, lads.

May 14th
RIP our resident Council poet, Carlotta Swan. Best known for her car-park couplet, 'Have you Paid & Displayed?' she was also responsible for 'Caution, Wet Floor,' - part of a sonnet sequence on the theme of slipping - and of course the astonishing haiku, 'No Right Turn.'

★

May 15th
As you know in 1972 the bypass became so busy we had to build a bypass bypass, & in 1989 a bypass bypass bypass. Sadly the bypass bypass bypass has now become so crowded that tomorrow we start work on a bypass bypass bypass bypass. Which for convenience sake we shall call Kevin.

May 17th
To the person who snapped me last night in the precinct, a simple explanation. Myself and the Mayor of Sleaford were on a wine-tasting tour of Chadwell. I stopped to buy flowers for Mrs. B. & slipped. Enough with the interrogation! – what is this, Line of f★★★ing Duty?! Back off.

May 20th
HURRAH!! Chadwell Wigs Ltd. has been named as Official
Supplier of hairpieces to TeamGB at the #Tokyo2020 Olympics!
The local firm will supply hair & false moustaches to all cyclists,
athletes, swimmers & weight-lifters. Here MD Tim Parslow
reacts with joy at the news. REJOICE!!!

May 21st
Oh yes, very funny. Ha bloody ha. Open my curtains this morning to see this, circling above Battley Towers. I know who it is. Ned Tench up at the aerodrome. He'll be laughing on the other side of his face when I table a motion this morning calling for his public execution.

May 22nd
CCTV footage of a giant ant in the underpass this afternoon. Apologies to everyone whose commute was interrupted. Now's not the time to play the blame game but it's fair to say Pest Control took its eye off the ball. Please don't let this put you off Chadwell's excellent late-night shopping.

May 23rd
Incensed. Apparently the Egyptian pyramid Chadwell Scout troop brought back from the Valley of the Kings 2 yrs ago, and which now stands in the park, has 'got to go back!' Chadwell is twinned with Cairo! It was a cultural exchange trip! We gave them 3 jars of our best chutney – a totally fair exchange in my view. I will fight this.

May 24th
Woken to a firestorm. Three of Chadwell's finest shove ha'penny players – Nigel 'Iron-hand' Fazackerly, Miriam 'The Wrist' Cornforth & Thaddeus Smash, are planning to form a #SuperLeague. I'm calling an emergency meeting in the snug bar of the Rampant Chimp. Updates to follow.

May 26th
Opened the new Birds of Prey Centre today.   Cluster-f★★★k. Whoever put it next to the Petting Zoo should be sectioned. To see 15 kestrels swoop like Messerchmitts & carry off 10 mice, 3 rabbits & a shrew is enough to chill the blood of the hardiest councillor. Heads will roll.

May 27th
This morning we gave a warm welcome to our our new Head of Diversity, Colonel Throgmorton Ashton-Corinthian Swaffham-Waverley. In his speech to the chamber today he pledged to have a Polynesian lollipop lady by 2023 or 'die by his own hand.'
Slightly dramatic, but we wish him well.

June 2nd

Bubbling with fury. Utter carnage at the village hall last night. Just been down to inspect the damage. Chairs thrown, bottles of vodka hurled through windows, ambulances called, police sirens flashing, ten arrested. I think it's fair to say there's a question-mark hovering over the future of Chadwell Boggle Club.

June 9th
Wonderful news! In response to the outpouring of public grief at the recent passing of our much-loved doorman Pat Cluck, we've decided to have him stuffed. His cheery smile will greet us at the revolving doors of the town hall forever. Welcome home, Pat!

June 28th
Just back from the Hotel Splendide where I was presenting the Sewage Worker of the Year Awards. Lifetime Achievement went to Lady Dowager Hermione Holstein III. The way she used to wriggle through those sewage pipes without so much as displacing her tiara was something to behold.

June 25th
Not again. Yet another Dalek thrown in the canal. That's the 23rd this month. The council will not tolerate abandoned mutant extra-terrestrials cluttering up our waterways. It was bad enough last year when 62 Cybermen were dredged from the ornamental pond. IT ENDS NOW!

June 30th
I along with thousands have been celebrating #WorldNakedGardeningDay. Only one little hitch - I didn't realise it had to be your own garden. I'd like to apologise to my neighbours the Braithwaites, who were startled this morning by the sight of me spraying their japonica.

July 3rd
EVENTS TODAY AT THE BANDSTAND:
1pm: Cage-fighter Hulk Musgrove reads from his latest book, 'The Wild Flowers of Norfolk.'
2pm the Rev. Waverley presents 'A History of Striptease,' with lantern slides.
3pm–Midnight: the Salvation Army Band plays the greatest hits of Rat Scabies.

July 8th
Delighted to announce that Chadwell Maze re-opens at the weekend! And can we PLEASE not rake up the fact that since 2012 six people have got lost and died in it? It was their own

stupid fault for not buying a map, and I can assure you that all the skeletons have been removed. Enjoy.

July 14th
A good time was had by all at the Church Fete on Sunday. A few eyebrows are being raised at the fact that I won the Bowling for a Pig, the Darts, the Golf, the Raffle, the Bingo, the Jiving Competition, and yes, the Ladies Skittles. Envy is not an attractive trait. Let it go.

July 20th
Delighted to welcome to the team our new Finance Director, Bobby Kipling. Don't be deceived by appearances – his double-entry book-keeping has won awards. Welcome aboard, Bobby.

July 28th
Mrs. B & myself having a quiet Sunday leafing through old photos. Happy memories of the council away-day to Scunthorpe in '72. That's us lounging on the diving board. Tina Bunt poses on the steps while nearby the Dalrymples discuss the finer points of the new ring-road proposals.

August 1st
Well the Chadwell Bank Holiday tradition of appointing a random resident Mayor for the day has been a giant cluster-f**k. Ted Quayle got roaring drunk in the Rampant Chimp & demolished the town hall. Relishing the next 3 months running the town from a portakabin.
I HATE YOU ALL!

August 3rd
I apologise on behalf of Chadwell Police who yesterday raided 5 houses & arrested 16 people for possession of Custard Creams. Inspector Pilcher issued the following statement: 'What can I say? I got all my laws mixed up. For some strange reason I thought biscuits were illegal and – well, the rest is history.'

August 14th
Disappointed. An illegal rave was broken up last night on the outskirts of Chadwell. Police arrested 200, some of whom were

dancing on the roof, and seized 15 kilos of cocaine. Frankly I expected better behaviour from the residents of Sunnylawns Care Home for the over-90's.

August 18th
FFS. This is Mrs. Clover. She's been walking round and round in a circle for three days. Thank God someone spotted her. She's now recovering in the Vicarage with a large brandy. I have only one thing to say to Bunt & Sons, road-painters. LAWYER UP, F***WITS, I'M COMING FOR YOU!!!

August 25th
The burden of leadership weighs heavy upon the shoulders of the great. Today I felt a wonderful kinship with my fellow leader President Biden as he signed executive orders on climate change, the Iran deal & Covid - while I approved a Frog Crossing in Canal Street. #InThisTogether

Sept.1st
Our motto here at Chadwell Council is FUN FUN FUN! Today, for example, it's #MothAwarenessDay, when we all dress up as

lepidoptera. This year the contest was won by our Catering Tsar Gregory Trowbridge.

But there's a serious side – moths keep the ecosystem going, or something.

Sept. 9th

I swept to power on a pledge to provide social housing to Chadwell's 3,000 homeless scuba divers. I'm thrilled to announce that the first phase of Chadwell's new affordable housing estate,

Stubley Meadows, has been completed. I will be holding an underwater press conference at 2pm.

Sept. 15th
WE'RE HIRING! A vacancy has arisen for a Council Continuity Person. Duties include making sure that when a councillor walks out of a room they come back in wearing the same clothes; if someone fluffs a speech they pick up from exactly the same point, etc. Free Luncheon Vouchers.

Sept.16th
A dark day in the history of Chadwell. The council have invoked the 25th Amendment of the town's byelaws and I have been suspended as your leader for seven days. Reeling with disgust. If a man can't go on a three-day bender and declare war on Luton I don't want to live in this country any more.

Sept. 24th
I swept to power on a platform of Truth. Two months ago I set up a committee to investigate what the council could do to prevent the Milky Way being pulled apart.

Today I was told - 'absolutely nothing.'
Sometimes the truth hurts.
I've stood the committee down.
I'm sorry.

Oct. 3rd
Ok. I know specialist shops are all the rage, but Tom Connell's
Ltd. in the High St. only selling rubber bands and yeast is frankly
taking the p**s. I've had a word with him and he says he 'hates
everything else.'

Oct. 16th
Not again. I can't take any more. ONCE AGAIN every single
creature in Chadwell Aquarium has escaped. 63 sea-urchins have
been spotted roaming the putting green and a squid is trying on
dresses in Top Shop. EVERYBODY IN!

Oct. 18th
People at the Battley Vaccination Centre have been surprised to
be greeted by an octopus. Let me explain. We were hoping that
'Olly' would be able to vaccinate 8 people in one go. Has it
worked? No. He's been a huge disappointment & will be
re-homed in Chadwell Aquarium tomorrow.

Oct. 20th
Long afternoon spent at the Vets. We had good old Benjy
micro-chipped, de-wormed, and vaccinated for distemper, rabies
and hepatitis. Some people don't think you should go to so much
trouble with a stick insect, but better safe than sorry, that's my
motto.

Oct. 21st
Ok. I'm all in favour of urban farms, but apparently there's a herd
of jersey shorthorns living in flat no 123 on the top floor of
Randall Tower. At milking time the lifts are crammed with

lowing bovines. I'm not even going to mention the corn-field in the lounge. It ends now!!

Oct. 23rd
I would like to apologise for the foul-mouthed argument at the Church Committee last night, in which I rounded on someone & called them a bloody %$"^?!★, a raving $£%"!!?, and a 'stupid £$%^&★$&★★%$?!'
Fair play, no Mother Superior should have to listen to that kind of language.

Oct. 24th
SPECIAL ANNOUNCEMENT: Chadwell Council has employed 73 Secretary Birds as Covid-Marshals. The Feather-Force, as I have called them, will patrol the streets & have the power to fine and make arrests. Any attempt to bribe them with birdseed will be against the law.

Nov. 1st
URGENT: After an investigation by our Standards Committee we've discovered that Reg Carstairs, our Education spokesman, is not just a puppet of rival administration Kettering District Council – he is also actually a puppet. He's been removed from office and thrown in a bin.

Nov. 12th
Quelle surprise. As the #LocalElections loom, once again I'm accused of 'buying votes' by inviting every resident to a gigantic free banquet tonight (Civic Centre, 7pm). Read my lips: IT'S MY AUNT'S BIRTHDAY! Is it my fault she has 10,000 friends? Electoral Commission – SWIVEL!!!

Nov. 29th
Brimming with pride that Chadwell is the first town in Britain to give votes to dogs. If successful, we will be rolling out votes for insects & amphibians by 2025. Who knows, by 2030 we may very well see a spider in power. Exciting times.

Nov. 30th
Great leaders handle election night in different ways. Me, I always go for a long solitary walk in the bluebell woods, sit on a tree-stump and read Wordsworth as the golden rays of the setting sun pierce the forest's mantle.
I then go and get pi★★ed in The Rampant Chimp.

Dec. 1st
Former Mayor of Chadwell Oswald Box (1883-1956). This photo was taken at his trial for attempting to poison the entire town. Extraordinarily, on his release, he was re-elected - on the

grounds that 'everyone deserves a second chance.' Tragically, he did it again. Different times.

Dec. 3rd
Delighted to be at the opening of a new branch of Eezi-Snooze Beds Ltd. in the High Street this evening. Manager Steve Bristow has really pushed the boat out, with balloons, local press & TV, clowns - he's even hired a fire-eater!

Sh★t. I knew the fire-eater was a mistake. No sooner had Mr. Bristow proclaimed 'I declare this shop OPEN!' when a jet of flame shot from the mouth of the Great Suprendo and a duck-down duvet turned into a fireball. Whole shop engulfed. Gone in minutes. And so to cribbage.

Dec. 6th
You make me sick. Moan moan bl★★dy moan. Yes, there's been a major water-leak in Brampton Road for the last three weeks. And yes, I've been charging tourists £10 a head to come and see the Chadwell Geyser. I ADAPT TO CIRCUMSTANCES! The leak continues. Deal with it, vermin.

Dec. 15th
Wonderful afternoon presenting awards at the BAFVA's, the British Academy Fruit & Vegetable Awards. Local man Lionel Crust won Best Supporting Onion, and Nora Lovelace won the Lifetime Achievement award for her pak choi. #ProudCouncillor.

Dec. 20th
As businesses begin to revive it's important to support local restaurants. I've been doing my bit by having four of these a day at Fat Bob's Guzzle Shack. I'm now 23 stone & was carried home yesterday in a wheelbarrow but by God I'm determined to re-inflate the local economy.

Dec. 21st
FANTASTIC NEWS! The Flying Shuttle pub re-opens tonight!
And I'm so glad they've done it up - last year it was looking a bit
run down.

Dec. 23rd
One of the greatest citizens in our town's history was the Bishop
of Chadwell, Augustus Crunch (1889-1956). Some are saying
that displaying his skeleton in a public building is 'morbid,' &
'upsetting.' WTAF? Unbelievable. He stays in the foyer of
Chadwell Primary School, end of. HAPPY CHRISTMAS!

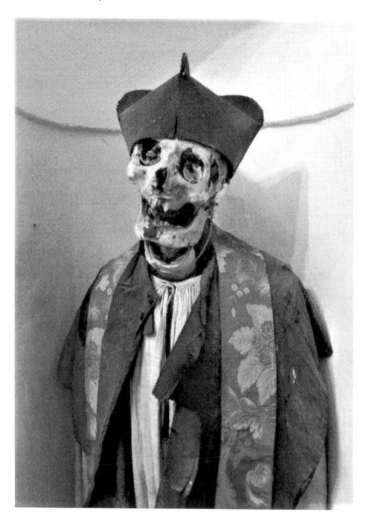

2023

Jan. 3rd
Ok. So Chadwell is #OpeningUp. I'll say one thing. This is the scene earlier at Nanny Watkin's Tea-Rooms. 600 people. There are only 4 tables! I haven't seen a mosh-pit like this since the Clash played Chadwell Town Hall. If this is 'exercising caution' my name's Rumplestiltskin.

Jan 7th
I have heartbreaking news. Edgar the Town Sloth has passed away peacefully after a long illness. He served Chadwell, here and abroad, for decades. Among his many achievements was implementing sloth-friendly access to the leisure centre, theatre & swimming pool. God speed, Edgar.

Jan. 12th

Incredible news. After ten long years, Chadwell Council's Scientist-in-Chief Agatha Wyoming has bred a dog with seven legs. This will revolutionise sheep-farming and surely put her in line for a Nobel Prize.

Jan. 17th

Can we all be a little more tolerant of baboons, please? Yes, it's an experiment to allow monkeys from Chadwell Safari Park to roam the town between the hours of 5pm–8pm. I am President of the Inter-Species Socialising Society, and as for your complaints, they make me sick and I reject them. The experiment continues. Have a good evening.

★

Jan. 18th
Not again.
EMERGENCY!!! Yet another tree has uprooted itself & run away from the Municipal Gardens. That's the tenth this month. Last week a Sycamore was seen sprinting down the A1.

It's very simple - if you see a tree fleeing from our beloved park, LASSOO THE WOODEN FUGITIVE!

Jan 30th
Happy memories of when David Bowie opened our church fete in 1986. Decent turn-out. The bric-a-brac stall sold out within seconds, the queue for the coconut shy stretched all the way to

the bypass and as for toffee-apples you couldn't get one for love nor money. Those were the days.

Feb. 1st
You disgusting savages. HOW MANY MORE TIMES? Earlier today this gate in Porlock Meadow was left unclosed. Sixteen sheep escaped and are roaming the precinct. MUST I LOSE MY LEISURE TIME TO THIS TORMENT?

Feb. 10th
Thrilled to announce that Chadwell's favourite theme park, Pallet-Land, IS OPEN! Meet all your favourite pallet characters – the cheeky Pallet-Imps, beautiful Penelope Pallet, & of course Old Father Pallet, dispensing his wisdom on everything from freight-charges to loading-regs.

Feb. 23rd

#Blessed. Today I was appointed United Nations Ambassador for the welfare of puppets. Too many abandoned puppets have to walk 15 miles to the nearest puppeteer. Chadwell's Puppet Hospital welcomes all marionettes - from glove to string - and our trained staff heal them and help them back into the community.

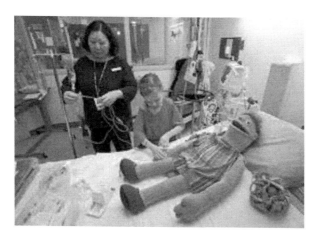

ANNOUNCEMENT: Owing to a double-booking tomorrow's performance by the Bolshoi Ballet of Tchaikovsky's Swan Lake will not take place at Chadwell Theatre but at Chicken Planet, Oildrum Lane. Chubby Sid's promised to rearrange the seating & tickets will include a free Bucket of Beaks.

March 18th

Mrs. B. & myself were leafing through old photos last night & came across this from the Chadwell Players Christmas panto, 1976. Far be it for me to boast but I became known as 'the finest Humpty Dumpty of his generation.' Not my words, the words of Ariadne Pipe in the Bugle. Happy days.

April 14th
Thrilled to unveil a new portrait of me in the town hall foyer.
Some critics are saying it resembles 'Napoleon' by Jacques David.
I can't see it myself, but the artist Ron Tyler said he 'painted me
as he sees me.' True, I gave him a few guidelines, but he's
captured me perfectly.

April 17th
Lovely relaxing Sunday. Mrs. Battley is in the kitchen being bold
with bananas and I'm kicking back on the sofa in the run-up to
watching Indoor Bowling with a plateful of Meat-Clown.
#Blessed.

April 23rd
Happy Straw Day everyone! - a tradition in which Chadwellians dress up as haystacks. We've forgotten the reason. Sadly, seconds after this was taken Mr. & Mrs. Bunt - below - were thrown into a field of cows. Mrs. Bunt was nibbled to within an inch of her life. Heads will roll.

May 1st
As Bob-a-Job Week comes to an end I'd like to thank Chadwell Cub Scouts for completing all those niggling little jobs around the town that needed doing. I'd particularly like to thank them for repairing the flyover and building a pedestrian underpass under Porlock Street. For their vital contribution to the town they have all been awarded their Infrastructure Badge. Wonderful. Hard to believe their average age is 10 and three quarters.

★

April 27th
Fears are growing over the sanity of our Finance Director Mrs. Runcible as she appears in the council chamber dressed as a lampshade. For the third time within a month. I'm no Hitler when it comes to dress-code but she's pushing my buttons.

May 3rd
A great day in the history of our beloved town! Today I officially launched HMS Battley, a 78,000-ton schooner with 10 heated pools & 48 indoor tennis courts. Its first voyage will take me to

the Caribbean, where I will cruise the islands preaching the gospel of fiscal prudence. REJOICE!

May 4th

Regular Wednesday evening chess match with next-door neighbour Tim Parker. I really thought I'd beat him tonight - but once again he smashed through my Sicilian Defence, rendered my bishops all but useless, and checkmated me in a matter of minutes. How a five year old boy has such command of the game is beyond me.

May 10th

Let me be clear. Did my deputy director of housing Marmaduke Brakespeare ride semi-naked on a donkey last night through the streets of Margate, singing I Am The Walrus?

Yes.

Do I stand by him as a man of principle, sobriety & honour?

I do.

The matter is closed.

PS. And PLEASE stop spreading this photo around. The man is a Rotarian.

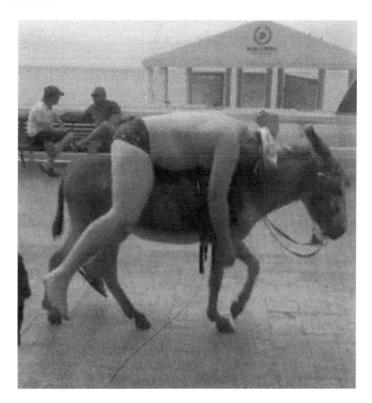

May 28th

Chadwell is blessed with many splendid tourist spots, not least our wonderful picnicking area overlooking the ring-road. With glorious views of our famous railings & Wally Crockett's Catering Van nearby, for a family day out it's hard to beat. CHADWELL IS OPEN FOR TOURISM

May 30th

Thrilled to announce that following his resignation from Amazon, Jeff Bezos will be taking over as chief fryer at Chicken Planet, Chadwell. 'I was shocked,' said manager Alan Cortez, 'but his CV's good & he begged me for a chance.' The online retail giant starts frying on Monday.

June 5th

Apologies for the display of insanity from Cedric Bloom the Housing Officer in the council chamber this morning. He's just back from a trip to Peru where apparently he ate the hallucinogenic plant Ayahuasca. We'll update you on his condition when we've got him down from the roof.

June 14th
I swept to power on a pledge to cancel all foreign debt to Chadwell. I can today announce that I have duly written off the £2.80 I paid to the Mayor of Zanzibar when he bought a cappucino on his visit to our town in 2008. LET'S CANCEL POVERTY!

June 25th
There's no finer sight in our town's calendar than the annual march through the precinct by the Rotary Club branch of Gay Pride. Here bank manager Winstanley Bradstock leads a regiment of Bowler-Hatted Pansexuals along Roper Street to the Municipal Gardens.

★

June 26th
Very pleased with the turnout today at the Municipal Gardens for
the Reverend Taylor's talk on Etruscan Pottery. We completely
ran out of lemonade & Mrs. Dalrymple's fairy-cakes were flying
off her trestle table.

July 12th
FFS. What began as a friendly visit
from the Mayor of Glossop ended
in an almighty cluster-f★★k. While
touring our local sweet factory he
slipped into a vat & was converted
into a chocolate rabbit. We've
returned him to Glossop in a box,
and await developments. And so to
whist.

August 14th
Thrilled to announce the release of my debut album, A Councillor's Dream. Featuring a selection of my favourite songs spanning many genres from sunshine-thrash to pastry-folk, the 12" vinyl, sponsored by Bisto, will be available wherever you get your gravy granules.

August 15th
Chadwell's local businesses go from strength to strength! Thrilled to announce that a new Cosmetic Brain Surgery has opened in

the High Street. Mrs. Battley has just booked in to have her neo-cortex buffed, her frontal lobes waxed, and her cerebellum lifted.

August 30th
Ok. A few answers.
Is Chadwell's nuclear plant next to a spider farm?
Yes.
Was a 50ft tarantula spotted in the High Street yesterday screaming 'death to all humans!'
Yes.
Is there a connection?
No.
Now can we please get on with our Sundays? I've got a Cub Scout Raffle to attend.

Sept.15th
HURRAH! When Mrs. Battley suggested we enter our dog Filligrew in the canine fancy dress contest as a door, I was a tad sceptical. He's only won! Very proud.

Sept. 20th
Just back from the annual Happiest Business-person of the Year Awards. And we have a worthy winner! With his cheery smile, infectious laugh & constant jokes, he entertains all who enter his premises. Congratulations to Ronald Footle of Baxter's Funeral Directors Ltd., Park Street.

Oct. 1st

To Bob Carter the bus driver of the number 32 who very kindly dropped me off on the top floor of Shadwell Buildings today in the High Street - thanks mate. The lift was out of order and I didn't fancy all those stairs, what with my knee being the way it is. Owe you one, Bob.

Oct. 8th
This week's local business plug is for DPD Logistics, Chadwell –
the only courier firm to offer an underwater delivery service.
Here a driver delivers a birthday present to a trout in the
Chadwell Canal.

Oct. 9th
A big day! Today Chadwell makes its bid to become Britain's
next #CityofCulture.

To that end we are sending one of the town's most notable artists
to Downing Street for the final selection process. The entire
borough wishes all the luck in the world to Benjy Sheldrake and
his naughty stork Pip. Quite thrilling to think he'll be performing
his fantastic 'drunken stork' routine in front of the Prime Minister.

Myself and Mrs. B. saw him at the British Legion and were in fits.
Go get 'em, Benjy!

Nov.1st
FFS. Tourists are complaining that the dolphins in Chadwell
Estuary are inflatable.
A few home-truths. Did the council advertise Dolphin-Watching
as a key tourist attraction?
Yes.
Did we say the dolphins were real?
No.
Read the small-print, f★★★wits.
Meanwhile, ENJOY THE F★★★ING PLASTIC DOLPHINS
AND STOP MOANING.

Nov. 2nd
Thrilled to be able to announce that Dudley the Massive Cat is once more on show in Chadwell Zoo. Measuring a mind-boggling 63ft, this titanic tabby, this mega-moggy, is the jewel in the crown of our tourist industry! COME ONE, COME ALL!

Nov. 7th
Thank you everyone who attended the bare-knuckle cage-fighting tournament this afternoon in the cellar of the Forlorn Weasel. The winner was Carlos 'Rabid Dog' Waverley who beat Tony 'The Doughnut' Muldoon. All proceeds go to Chadwell Crochet Club.

Nov. 8th
I'm proud to announce that in the last 3 months I've created 1.2 million local jobs. An extraordinary achievement, given the

population of Chadwell is only 15,000. This means that everyone now has 80 jobs.

I know. I didn't think this through. Leave it with me.

Nov. 15th

Earlier today reports came in that two canine Jedi's had risen from the municipal lake to attack Chadwell. We called press, local TV – even Beth Rigby from Sky turned up!

They were Ron Fossett's labradors after a swim. Thanks for wasting my day. Can you please just stop this?

Nov. 25th

Councillor Cecil Trowbridge addressing the chamber yesterday. It was slightly tricky to decipher but the gist of his oration was that our town is 'under threat from the Lizard People of Kettering.' Frankly I think his days as Head of Well-Being are numbered.

Nov. 28th
Just back from a wonderful presentation by the Chadwell Police Dog Display Team. Tyson on the left demonstrated rudimentary

techniques in combating international cyber-fraud, while Fifi Trixibelle in the middle delivered an enthralling lecture on advanced forensics.

HENRY KISSINGER
1923-2023

Nov. 29th
#HenryKissinger & I were firm friends. He often sought my advice on political matters. After one 'phone chat in the late 60s he embarked on the controversial bombing of Cambodia. I'd actually advised him to 'bomb Camberley,' but the line was bad. How we laughed afterwards. RIP.

Dec. 3rd

This evening it was my honour to turn on Chadwell's Christmas lights in the precinct.

I was greeted with this.

I refuse to show the display which formed the words 'Battley is a c★★k.'

Be in no doubt I have ordered a full independent inquiry. I will not tolerate luminous filth.

Dec. 11th

Oh God, not again. Our head of accounts Mr. Carisbrooke is having another one of his episodes. This photo was taken outside Matalan an hour ago. We all know the drill - keep away from him and whatever you do don't throw him a ball of wool. He'll be alright in the morning.

Dec. 15th
WE'RE HIRING! The council is on the look-out for a new Witchfinder General. Bob Pump has served us well for 15 yrs but has decided to call it a day & open a tuck shop. His are tricky shoes to fill - under his leadership 163 people were arrested, tried, and rightly executed.
Is this you? Post incl. gym membership & pension. DM me.

Dec. 18th
I swept to power on two major commitments: to build the ring-road, and to increase tolerance of public nudism. Yet tonight I was cautioned by a constable for strolling down the vegetable

aisle of the Co-op as naked as God made me. ARE WE GOING BACKWARDS, CHADWELL? WELL ARE WE?!

Dec. 31st
As ever, the Rotary Club has done us proud. Our heartfelt thanks go to Mrs. Penelope Soper for allowing us to hold the New Year firework display in her back garden. Sorry your house went up in flames Penny, but I'm sure you'll agree it was worth it.
HAPPY NEW YEAR CHADWELLIANS!

Jan. 4th
VICTORY! Following a 5 yr undercover operation my anti-corruption team has smashed Chadwell's biggest chutney cartel. This is 100-year old Felicity Burrows, known to her henchwomen as 'Fingers Fliss.' For 30 years she ran an illegal chutney empire from her cottage in Bluebell Crscent. Last night she was in a cell. Good. Chadwell can breathe again wit this vile felon behind bars.

Jan. 5th
Me patrolling the town centre earlier today with 14 Chieftan Tanks as part of the council's Say No to Litter campaign. It gives me no pleasure to say that 48 litterbugs were shot. Hopefully the message has got through. WELL HAS IT, CHADWELL?!

Jan. 23rd
It's time I explained my fortnight's absence. I have a rare condition that means over-eating affects my height, not my weight. Recently I ballooned to a grotesque 7ft 6. After a stay in the Priory I am now down to a respectable 6ft 4.
But it's not over.
Pray for me, Chadwell.

Jan. 29th
A sad day in the history of Chadwell. The council's been ordered to 'update its healthcare provision.' So it is with great reluctance that I must announce that the Leper Colony will be closed.

A great shame. They loved living on that island on the Municipal Lake.
And so to golf.

Feb. 7th
A blast from the past! As a catalogue model (that's me in the middle) I met two lifelong friends. We may have been modelling fashion but our hearts were in local politics. George Cork on the left now runs zebra crossings & Teddy Cinnamon is currently juggling footpaths & sewage.

Feb. 15th
An incredible 68 million people have visited Chadwell's Cup-a-Soup Museum since April, putting it in the top 10 visitor attractions in the world, just below Disneyland & the Sistine Chapel. Includes the famous 'Mulligatawney Ride of Death.' Why not visit today?
#ProudCouncillor

Feb. 20th

Full of regrets today. I had high hopes for our council Drug Tsar, Lancelot Yolk. 6 months ago he pledged to 'cleanse Chadwell of drug abuse.' Yesterday he was spotted running naked through the municipal gardens off his head on ket & meow-meow shouting 'I am the God of hellfire.' HR have been informed.

Feb. 27th

It has come to my attention that the Council's Animal Welfare Officer, Botticelli Truscott, is the author of a pamphlet published in 1973 entitled 'Dodos - I'm Glad They're Gone.' Truscott has been suspended pending further investigations.

March 2nd

I can't take any more. The council's Chief Finance Officer, Bronwen Hippocampus, has been put on probation after the publication of her memoirs, 'Dogging is my Life.'
IS THERE ANYONE ON THIS COUNCIL WHO ISN'T A DEGENERATE?
And so to badminton.

March 7th

Just back from a moving #RemembranceDay ceremony at Chadwell's Tomb of the Unknown Soldier. The afternoon was spoiled somewhat by the dramatic news that DNA analysis has identified the unknown soldier as Obergruppenfuhrer Siegfried Muller of the Waffen SS. A review of future ceremonies is underway.

March 9th

With heavy heart I must announce an attempt has been made on my life. Three days ago a tyre was dropped on my head from the multi-storey car-park. Two Russians were identified, who claim they were in Chadwell visiting our world famous Thimble Museum. I'm coming for you, Putin.

March 10th
At long last the newly-refurbished Battley Theatre is re-opening!
The inaugural production is a major new musical, 'Battley!' –
tracing the story of my life from a humble terraced house in
Kettering to the Himalayan summits of provincial government.
Starring Michael Ball as me.

March 12th
It is with great regret that as part of the financial cutbacks the
Council Mascot – currently a Shire Horse – is being replaced by a
Hydro-Thermal Worm only visible with an electron microscope.
Come and meet Lucy the Worm tomorrow when she'll be
turning on the Christmas lights.

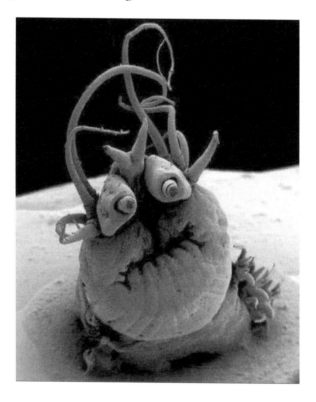

March 28th
Today we said goodbye to our head of Parks & Open Spaces, Benjamin Ninepence. In an unfortunate turn of events we discovered he'd been dead for five years. We just thought he was very quiet. Still, we had a whip round for him, and signed his card. Enjoy your 'retirement,' Benjy.

April 13th
Today I was proud to hand over the keys to the tenants of Chadwell's 1000th council house, built by Horace Futtock Ltd. And to those complaining that the 'doorway's in the wrong place,' I want to state for the record that I didn't know Futtock is cross-eyed. My hands are clean.

April 14th
I am not ashamed to confess I am shedding a manly tear. But they are tears of gratitude & humility that fall softly on my municipal trousers. For today I heard that the funds for the permanent statue of myself have finally been released.

★

I can honestly say this is the greatest day of my life. It has been a long and bitter struggle, a battle marked by ghastly accusations such as 'you don't deserve a 600ft tall memorial, you bast★★d,' 'you are a massive t★t' – and other sundry slanders that have slid from me like droplets from the feathers of a mallard. But at last the people have spoken.

It is with a lump in my throat that I unveil the first image of the monument to myself that will overlook our beloved town:

And so ends these humble chronicles. We have come a long way, my people, through the best of times and the worst of times. I lay down my fountain pen - a Parker Vector 2000 with medium gold nib, price £17.99 from W.H. Smiths - and gaze thoughtfully out of my office window at the re-cycling bins and Nobby Asterix the mad busker screeching out four choruses of *Smells like Teen Spirit* to the empty wastelands fringing the gasworks.

The sun is setting over our beloved Chadwell. But as sure as night follows day, day will follow night, and tomorrow there will follow another day and a new dawn and then another night – you get the picture.

God bless you all, and God bless our beloved borough.

(NB. I NEVER SAID the money for a new orphanage was "ring-fenced," so BACK OFF!)